Practical and Professional Ethics

VOLUME ONE
The Primer of Applied Ethics

Practical and Professional Ethics Series

Vol. 1: The Primer of Applied Ethics
Vol. 2: Environmental Ethics
Vol. 3: Bio-Medical Ethics
Vol. 4: Educational Ethics
Vol. 5: Economic and Business Ethics
Vol. 6: Socio-Political Ethics

About the Author

Mr. Debashis Guha, teaches Ethics and Phenomenology and Existentialism in the Post Graduate Department of Philosophy, Ranchi University, Ranchi. After doing masters course in Philosophy from Delhi University in 1980, he was conferred the Ph.D. degree of Jadavpur University in 1988. Dr. Guha takes interest in Philosophy of Religion, Social and Political Philosophy, Philosophy of Science and Analytic Philosophy. He taught at the undergraduate level in a constituent college of Ranchi University from 1981 to 1989 and was then asked to serve the Post Graduate Department. Dr. Guha is teaching Ethics for twenty-four years. He was awarded the Visiting Associateship of the U.G.C. (1994-96) in Jadavpur University, Calcutta, where he worked out *An Inquiry into the cases of Pain and Suffering,* which awaits publication. He was further awarded U.G.C.'s Major Research Project (1997-2000) on *Applied Ethics in Indian Context,* which has been now shaped in Six volumes, of which the present work is the first one under the series: **Practical and Professional Ethics**. Dr. Guha has fourteen papers to his credit. He has presented philosophical papers in different Seminars, Symposia and Congress, two of them were presented in International Congress; one in the Platinum Jubilee Celebrations of the Indian Philosophical Congress, 2000-01, and the other in the XVth International Congress of Aesthetics in Tokyo, Japan in 2001. During his Major Research Project work, Dr. Guha has talked to many people from different walks of life, interviewed them and also arranged ethical dialogues leading to resolution of value-laden practical problems of urgency. Dr. Guha envisions peoples' participation in Practical and Professional Ethics.

Practical and Professional Ethics

Volume-One

The Primer of Applied Ethics

DEBASHIS GUHA

CONCEPT PUBLISHING COMPANY, NEW DELHI-110059

Cataloging in Publication Data—DK
Courtesy: D.K. Agencies (P) Ltd. <docinfo@dkagencies.com>

Guha, Debashis.
Practical and professional ethics / Debashis Guha.
v. cm.
Includes bibliographical references.
Includes indexes.
Contents: v. 1. The primer of applied ethics — v. 2. Environmental ethics
ISBN 8180693147 (set)
ISBN 8180693155 (v. 1)
ISBN 8180693163 (v. 2)

1. Applied ethics. 2. Professional ethics. I. Title.

DDC 170 22

ISBN 81-8069-314-7 (Set)
ISBN 81-8069-315-5 (Vol. I) (H.B)
ISBN 81-8069-355-4 (Vol. I) (P.B)

Series

First Published 2007

Published and Printed by
Ashok Kumar Mittal
Concept Publishing Company
A/15-16, Commercial Block, Mohan Garden
New Delhi-110059 (INDIA)

Phones : 25351460, 25351794
Fax : 091-11-25357103
Email : publishing@conceptpub.com

To My Parents

Foreword

Present-day civilization, even our own culture, is very complex. Philosophical analysis of man's achievements, never very popular, should be encouraged. But if a deeper study of human thinking and behaviour is initiated, one is immediately confronted with what could be called our "value" system.

Applied Ethics tries to elucidate the underlying concepts involved in our value system. May the vast experience of the author, as exemplified in this work, act as a step forward towards a wider reflection on our world of "values". Few of us make the necessary effort to dig and find the hidden treasure, the real wisdom that will give our lives its true worth.

Ranchi
August 18, 2005

Fr. C. De Brouwer
Retd. Professor of Physics,
St. Xavier's College,
Ranchi

Preface

Applied Ethics is a new passion among ethicists and many non-philosophers worldwide. It is rapidly catching up the Indian intelligentsia, thanks to a fashionable new *mantra* "values", as if, "values" has been suddenly discovered as something worth discussing. Interestingly, philosophers' as well as non-philosophers' hue and cry about 'values' often end up in discussing "human values", "moral values", "ethical values" and so on but not what we know as "axiological study of value". Given this ethical focus, we now tend to care about the ethical or the moral value of a decision taken by different people, and we care about several value-laden practical problems troubling us. With this, we enter into the passion called "practical ethics" (sometimes called "applied ethics"). Nevertheless, to our great astonishment, many of us wonder, what is "practical ethics"? How can ethics, which is within philosophy, be "practical" or "applied"? The idea is that philosophy and ethics, which are theory-laden, cannot be "applied" or "practical". In addition, if it makes some sense, one should let others know about it. I have this task before me. The Primer of Applied Ethics thus aims at establishing that Applied Ethics does make a sense, it is within Ethics proper and it does not malign ethics. This is so important for me because either in India, as beginners in this field, we are facing skeptics (particularly the old-fashioned analysts) who would like to whisk away this rubbish or we are having those philosophers who eke out a small pittance for this apparently important thing. Both have a problem, that is, they have a misconception about model of ethical application and tend to believe that applied or practical ethics is either rubbish or something which is important but we know not what. In the book I will deal with the models of ethical application, try to show the sense in which ethical application is within ethics, and that it is not a rubbish effort. In doing so, I would argue in favour of a model, which has been effective in ethical resolution. This will provide a basis of applied ethics education in India I believe because without a proper knowledge of the basics of applied ethics, applying ethics is a non-starter.

DEBASHIS GUHA

Contents

Introduction

The main objective of this Primer is to provide the philosophers and the non-philosophers with a clear idea about at least two things. One is that though the case of applied ethics is not so well-established even after forty odd years, and ethical skeptics are not overdoing when they are providing their best arguments (they think so) to dislodge the claim that applied ethics is within ethics, ethicists are able to provide counter arguments against the skeptics and firmly establish the case of applied ethics. This is extremely important for ethicists because any details about how ethics has to be applied, makes no sense if one does not clearly justify why applied ethics is a sensible discourse within ethics. This is all the more important for the non-philosophers who will be benefited by the views of the antagonists and the protagonists regarding the case of applied ethics and shall come to know more about the nature of ethics and its tasks along with the nature of applied ethics and its tasks. In fact, the non-philosophers either who are emotional followers of applied ethics or who are fashionable followers of the same should be given a clear idea about what is applied ethics. If we do not undertake this task, applied ethics in the end may have some such philosopher and non-philosopher friends who have a tendency to make new friends for they are attractive but they are fooled when someone accuses them of making a bogus friendship. So first, we must have enough reason in favour of applying ethics rather than jump on to apply ethics.

Another clear idea this Primer attempts to give to our philosopher and non-philosopher friends is how ethics ought to be applied. Because once we know what applied ethics is, we should know about the proper methodology of application of ethics. Not only this, considering real-life application of ethics is important as well, for which, a methodology that works is needed. However, the tragedy is that once we have misconceptions about the nature of applied ethics, we are almost sure to misconceive how to apply ethics. In addition, the misconception has been an unfortunate thing for the young applied ethics. Certainly, a lot of confusion about the method of ethical application shrouds the minds of the ethical skeptics and the minds of not-so-skeptical-but-less-informed-philosophers-and-non-philosophers. The confusion is but natural because some of the traditionalists in applied ethics have propagated some such methods of application, which are highly, dubitable. The doubt is really about the possibility of such application. Moreover, a subject like ethics, which has been dominantly discussed within philosophy as theory-laden and involving mental-gymnastics, cannot be suddenly accepted as "practical" or "applied" if the method is not clearly stated and well justified. In order to perform this task of justification, we have to explain clearly the basics of different models advocated so far, their nuances and then go for thorough ethical analysis of these models to provide the friends of applied ethics with a proper methodology apart from sound reason to stand their ground firmly when their rationality is challenged.

Hence, both the objectives of writing this Primer may be rolled into one to call it "justificatory" because without justifying the need of applying ethics and the method of applying ethics, a venture into the discussion of the ethic of euthanasia and abortion and so on is needless. Nevertheless, to our great surprise, a large number of books on applied ethics neglect this basic task of justifying the case of applied ethics as a sensible discussion within ethics. However, this is so important for our readers. In fact, a large number of books give a wrong impression about applied ethics in starting with explanation of normative theories, which are portrayed as tools of ethical application, and then a case or practical value-laden case is considered for moral resolution through ethical application of these tools by expert ethicists. This is peculiar. Why should applied ethics be like this? Readers of this primer may discover how applied ethics should be approached *de novo*.

One must not have an idea that Primers are for novices. In fact, this Primer is for the beginners of ethics and applied ethics, as well as for trained philosophers and ethicists. The Primer is also for those non-philosophers who have some knowledge of ethics and applied ethics. To address to these readers, I want to stick to the basics stated above in chapters 1, 2 and 3. In chapter 1, I shall deal with nature, tasks and branches of ethics. In doing so, I shall justify that, applied ethics is within ethics. The arguments in favour of such justification mainly aim at dislodging the ethical skeptics and novices in the field of ethics nurturing several misconceptions. Chapter 2 shall concentrate more on the nature, tasks and need of professional ethics and its relation with applied ethics. In due course, it will be justified that professional ethics is within ethics as well. I would like to justify that to talk about a well-justified model of applying ethics is sufficient to understand how professional ethical problems should be resolved. Chapter 3 is more specific about the need for a proper model of ethical application. The discussion again focuses on the several misconceptions about application of ethics and about how ethics has to be applied. After going through the archaic models and their defects, I shall come to justify the model proposed by me. Further, in Chapter 4, I shall elaborate the nature of a value-laden practical problem awaiting ethical application for a constructive ethical resolution and formulation of decision-making rules for concerned professionals. However, I shall here concentrate on what has been done in India. Yet, it may serve as a fair sample of ethical application elsewhere by considering a number of value-laden practical problems. In Chapter 5, I shall discuss about the aim and need of teaching ethics and applied ethics. Naturally, it will be important to tell about models of teaching ethics and applied ethics. Finally, I would like to write about the relevance and prospects of applying ethics in the concluding chapter.

The work has been completed with the generous funding of the Indian Council of Philosophical Research, for which, I thank all related people of the Council. For study materials, I am indebted to Mr. G. Kumarappa of the National Library, Calcutta. I am thankful to Mr. Arun Kumar Verma and Mr. Sanjay Kumar Singh for typing the manuscript with great care.

1

The Nature and Tasks of Ethics

We take a calculated risk when we attempt at discussing some such thing, which is relatively less known to us or something about which many of us are skeptical. In philosophy we have a branch called "Ethics" which is ill-fated in so far as many philosophers still know little about what are its tasks and many philosophers are skeptical about normative ethics and applied ethics as forming a coherent whole called "ethics". Really speaking, we cannot straightaway jump to consider the justification of normative ethics and applied ethics as branches within ethics and to show that the tasks of ethics are at least three and not one. This is because one, who has no idea about what is "ethics", would not understand the above intricacies. Therefore, instead of addressing to the above problems, we should better focus our attention on the nature of ethics. This is particularly important for non-philosophers who take some interest in ethics and yet they are not so well trained in that field. However, that does not prevent them from knowing what ethics is. As for philosophers who are well trained, needs an introduction because many so-called well-trained people nurture misconceptions about what is ethics, what are its tasks and what are the branches of ethics. Anyway a discussion about the nature of ethics is very important for all interested parties, the philosophers and the non-philosophers.

Interestingly, to consider this fundamental question is to fall in line with the basic spirit of philosophy, which is a critical analysis of a number of fundamental philosophical concepts. When we start analyzing what is "ethics", we are in fact analyzing not a thing, a fact, an event, rather, a concept that is philosophical or pertaining to a branch of knowledge called Philosophy. Similarly, to consider what is "philosophy" is to consider a concept "philosophy" within Philosophy to analyze for its clear meaning. Nevertheless, to analyze the meaning of "philosophy" and "ethics" is essentially meta-philosophical and meta-ethical respectively because here we are undertaking a linguistic task primarily. Hence, to know what "ethics" is, is to fall in line with the extremely important task of ethics, viz., its metaethical task. Clearly, this question is a conceptual question, a question about language and not a factual question. However, there is no need to think that this is ethics, i.e., a theoretical jugglery with language to know what the meaning of such and such concepts is. Ethics is something more. Nevertheless, to state what is more in ethics will be too preposterous, particularly for those non-philosophers who are not likely to understand these intricacies. Hence, an elliptical way would be best in this case, and I believe, as we progress, our trained philosophers might appreciate this elliptical approach. This is to consider at the outset what ethics is not. One simple reason to take this longer turn is that even our non-philosopher friends risk a few conjectures about the nature of ethics and morality and may tend to stick to a fixed notion that 'this is what is ethics'. Let us first analyze what are the popular notions of non-philosophers and philosophers about the nature of ethics. I will then try to show why such and such things are not ethics. Finally, perhaps as an anti-climax, we will discover what the tasks of ethics are.

The first conception, rather misconception about ethics is that it is a subject that lays down set of prohibitory rules or codes, particularly those about sex and about other funs. We have to show that ethics is not about laying such rules. Non-philosophers and some philosophers tend to believe that "ethics" is what "morality" is and it is medieval Puritanism because it is very disturbing for fun loving human nature as far as it lays down several prohibitory rules. These rules are often puritanical because they are meant to purify our blemished characters, our darker souls. In addition, this darkness is mainly owing to our uninhibited sexual desires, other infatuations and greed. Therefore, ethics (or popularly called, morality) is about prohibiting sex particularly and other gross funs generally. Often a modern man talks about the "valuelessness", the "moral degradation" and "ethical corruption" these days. What they have in mind most of the time are gross things like homosexuality, blue films, rape, lesbianism, polygamy, polyandry and so on, and they think that ethics or morality has the burdensome task to lay rules to prohibit such gross things; otherwise, the society will crumble to dust. Ethics is thus the safety valve of sensible people in the society. It is not that ethics will teach us to shun sex totally and become freaks of nature rather, it will teach us to behave when we are involved in sex matters. It should be refined, if there is one such thing as a "refined sex behaviour". So ethics or morality is the name of setting high moral standards for a healthy sexual life, is one of the beliefs, and it is grossly mistaken for more reasons than one. First, ethics, morality and moral science are not the same things because ethics is what a branch of philosophical discussion is and although it has something to do with individual morality and public morality, it is something more. Hence, ethics is not merely setting norms of rules or codes for individual and public moral behaviour. Second, even morality cannot be relegated to something concerned with sex prohibitions because sex corruption may be one aspect of blemished moral life or rather an immoral life at best but it cannot be the whole story. Private and public morality may consider several aspects of human voluntary actions, sex corruption may be one but not all. Next, ethics and even morality cannot be about "sex" or about "prohibiting gross sex" because a scientific discussion about sexual life of human beings is essentially a factual study involving physiology, biology, psychology, sociology and so on but not ethics, which has nothing to do with this factual problem. Sex in itself does not pose any specific ethical issue and does not pose a moral issue. It is not an ethical issue because it is factual (scientific) issue and the clarification of its meaning or the conceptual analysis of "sex" is not undertaken in ethics. Similarly, "sex" in itself does not raise any moral issue because it is essentially biological and not moral. But some voluntary practices of "sex" may raise serious ethical as well as moral questions like, "Should right of the gays be protected?", "What is moral in protecting the right of the sex-workers?" etc. However, analyzing such questions is different from merely laying down rules or codes to prevent some fun people want to have. Hence, ethics and morality may have some questions to consider about sexual practices in society but this is not what ethics and morality are all about, and to prescribe don'ts to stop bad sex in society is not the business of the subject called "ethics". It may be the business of social hygiene nevertheless and a great burden for health administrators and health workers. It is better, therefore, to stop thinking that ethicists are what we call "moralists" in society who are our self-declared local-guardians to prevent us from "sex" and/or "bad sex" by setting rules or commands.

Nevertheless, can ethics act a guardian to provide behaviour cues to individuals in tricky situations? In fact, it is another gross error to think that ethics is some kind of behavioural science as far as it lays down clear-cut rules of human behaviour, which are pragmatic rules of thumb in problematic situations in daily life. This is to imagine that we have thumb-rules for human decent behaviour. However, what this "decency" is difficult to ascertain because we may think that it is decent to follow rules of our guardians, our parents, our teachers and so on. However, is it proper to think that when external authorities lay down rules, they become ethical rules? We can easily have instances of parental advices, which are believed to be decent or ethical by some and not so ethical by others. The definition of such a decency changes with changing time, place and societies. Moreover, family and social etiquettes are far from what we call ethical codes. Because those are patterns of social behaviours that are valued to be decent within period by a handful of people, while social disagreements may be sharp. How should we act in such and such situations in society may not be authoritative guide at all. This is because authorities are external sources of decision making which tend to impose ethical ideals in the form of fixed set of rules, without caring for our moral freedom and urge for moral disagreement. Such authoritative rules may be prejudiced, subjective, and orthodox and suffer from fixity of belief. Hence, they are not ethical. An ethical principle demands generality, acceptability and stands as an ideal within the changing times. Parental or any subjective or school-code-book type guidelines hinder individual's moral decision making, encourages absolutism, and are, therefore, not ethical themselves. Therefore, ethics cannot be something setting behavioural cues for all people, for all times in the form of cut-dried thumb rules to pick out one advice and reject other advices. We have to understand that whenever we speak of ethical first principles, they are ideals or ends of our voluntary actions but not rules of thumb, which are means to achieve an end. Therefore, ethics cannot act a guardian or a caretaker of individual and public behavioural decencies. It is due to this that ethics as a subject has to be distinguished from moral science because the latter deals mainly with individual and public etiquette and with the norms to lead a so-called decent life. Ethics may be rather called moral philosophy, i.e. a philosophical discussion pertaining to morality or a philosophical critique of morality, which is far from being laying down thumb-rules of behaviour. However, which philosophical discussion pertains to morality? We had an instance of one such discussion, viz. the linguistic discussion of the analysis of ethical language. Now we have another one, i.e., discussion of ethical principles. To discuss about the nature of the principles and about how they are different from parental rules or secondary rules of human behaviour. Another one may be how many ethical principles can be conceived and what they are. Most interesting question is, has ethics nothing to do with resolving value-laden practical problems? This last question will emerge in another context. For the present, let us move on to see what else not ethics is.

What follows from our earlier discussion about external authority as setting moral codes for human behaviour is that even religious codes may not be the same as ethical codes. However, there are many who believe that ethics is all religion or that ethics makes sense only in the context of religion. Those who hold this opinion argue that the analysis of the meaning of ethical language is possible only because of religion or that ethical language may be explained in terms of religious language. For instance, the central concept of ethics, which is concept of "good", may be explained in terms of "what God approves". Hence, the statement, "honesty is good" may be explained as "honesty is approved by God". This transmutation of one language into another is tricky. How do we say that "good" and "what is approved by God" are the same things when they are so appallingly different? "Good" is an ethical predicate widely used to evaluate human actions, decisions etc. in the ethical context. It is an evaluative term serving a unique function in ethical context. At best, we may say that it is closer to what we call "worth" in the ethical discussion. Nevertheless, how can it be replaced by "that which is approved by God"? Problem is, if "honesty" is "that which is approved by God" then, is "honesty" good and thus "approved by God" or "God approves honesty" to make it "good". If the value or worth of "honesty" lies in God's approval, then the particular deed is extrinsically good and not valuable-in-itself, which is a repugnant idea because if "honesty" is extrinsically valuable, i.e., may be good depending on an approval then, God approves bad things as well because "honesty" at times turns out to be fateful for some persons and therefore, not good at all. Therefore, we have to accept that "honesty" can be both good and bad, and approved by God. On the other hand, if "honesty" is intrinsically good, and, therefore, approved by God then, one has to rule out the possibility of "honesty" being "bad" at times. To rule out this possibility is to say that we know that "honesty" has an absolute value but how we know all that is difficult to ascertain. One may argue that the absolute "goodness" of "honesty" is intuitively known and following the same line, one may say that "honesty" is "God's approval", is also known intuitively to us. However, how do we intuitively know that we have an intuitive capacity to know such things? The regress is alarming. In fact we forget while analyzing ethical language in terms of religious language that "honesty" being evaluated as either "good" or "bad", is a human affair, and that its goodness and badness does not depend on what we say or what we evaluate rather what follows from the acceptance of a standard or criterion of evaluation. With this we come to the talk of moral standards or norms, which is another important task of ethics, it comes within what we call "normative ethics". Therefore, what theists have in mind is not transmutation of language but moral evaluation based on a criterion of moral evaluation. The criterion is, however, an external criterion, an Absolute Authority of God. So what they say is that "Honesty is good" means honesty is of moral worth in so far as we accept the truism that "God is the measure of all goodness and badness" or that "God's approval is the only standard of morality". This raises many problems. For every normative theory, we should ask for justification because simple presupposition or dull acceptance cannot be a proper justification. The justification provided is the intuitive justification once again, and we may skip repeating the obvious problem with this justification. Nevertheless, we may add to this another one. Why should our intuitions be similar? What is wrong with a Buddhist intuition that not God's approval rather other Authority, the Authority of the Buddha is the basis of ethical approval? The problem in reality is why should there be necessarily a uniform intuition about an Authority, viz., God. There is perhaps no ground but arrogant orthodoxy to support that only God's authority is the basis of morality. However, the religious people may forget petty differences to assert that after all some Authority, personal or impersonal, which is of course sacrosanct and true, must be the basis of moral evaluation. Hence, if not God, a religious document may be the basis of declaring "honesty" as "good". Clearly, the basis is external and it robs off the vital freedom of moral doer and moral evaluator. Every time I think that "honesty" is "good", I have to imagine another source external to me, which serves as the basis of evaluation. This is not a happy situation for a moral evaluator turns out to be a mere spectator and his rationality is at best a damp squib because what it can do best is to justify that God or an Authority is necessary and sufficient ground for moral evaluation. Moreover, external authorities are many and not one (as I have mentioned earlier), each standing firmly on its own ground for fictitious reasons, and we have hardly any option but to choose one arbitrarily, (without reason). So authoritative standard of moral evaluation turns out to be arbitrary choice and are in reality non-moral or transcending morality because any assumption of an alien standard is clearly outside morality. We may thus conclude that ethics and religion is not the same thing or ethics is not religion. One has to understand, therefore, that obeying divine commands and Authoritative commands is not necessarily the same as behaving ethically and the talk of such commands is not necessarily ethics-talk.

Our discussion about religion has revealed some important things, (a) there can be no absolutely true, sacrosanct moral authority or authoritative standard which can replace the whole gamut of morality; (b) ethics is thus not social, cultural, economic, religious dogma; (c) ethics is not what is tradition, a custom, a set of beliefs; and (d) ethics is neither arbitrary subjective construction of an external standard without any rational justification nor is it arbitrary subjective acceptance of an external standard without rational justification. From this we understand that it will be a gross mistake to believe that what we call "ethics" is a discipline which tells us about local, social, racial and other dogmas pertaining to what we should do and what we should not do. If this were the case then any external standard of do's and don'ts cannot be the same as what we call "ethics". The reasons are mainly two. One is that the dogmatic standards cannot serve as the general standards of morality which are well justified and transcends time, space, locale and whims. Another point is that these standards being external sources of morality, stands against the moral doer and evaluator's inherent moral freedom. This urge for generalization in ethics may be resolved by saying that if the basic spirit of external standard is clearly spelt out; we are really speaking about a generalized theory, called "relativism" or "ethical relativism". This turns out to be the only basis of morality or to be more sweeping; ethics is "relative social, cultural, political, religious and other dogma". Is it not true that the ethic of people is the ethic of the present social, cultural, political, and religious dogmas? To this, one may add that ethics is also "subjective" in so far as ethics is relative to what individual's value-systems are within a space and time, and which may be either influenced or completely independent of the value-system of the society or the nation. Therefore, ethics is either a social dogma or an individual dogma or both. However, ethics is not merely an individual or social dogma, nor is it both. To be clearer, ethics is not merely a body of relative or subjective dogmas. Let us justify this.

The confusion in the minds of the relativists and the subjectivists is clear. We had a glimpse of it at the beginning of the discussion. They forget that their assumption that "ethics is but relative or subjective dogmas" becomes a generalized ethical theory or an ethical standard by itself. Interesting is to notice that this becomes an Authority for the proponents. So ethical relativism and ethical subjectivism does not rule out the absoluteness of the moral standard as well the absoluteness of the notion that there is at one time, one subjective and/or social dogma which is the standard of morality. In the grab of relativism, what do we find? Do we not get an idea that "morality is necessarily relative to person, time and place". This is nurturing an absolute idea that there can be but only one criterion of moral evaluation, and it is, an authority. We know by now what are the defects of such thinking and if we stress much on absolutism, we tend to forget the basic relativism in ethical standards. Ethical relativism is self-defeating if it declares that only one generalized ethical standard is possible whatever may be cases of changing locale and changing people. If this goes too far, ethics turns out to be a non-optioned subject because here we have to believe but one thing and that is, people's ethics or people's value-system is the gift of present dogmas. Nevertheless, ethics is not non-optional, it is in fact multi-optional and we know about it as we progress through the path of normative ethics. Interestingly, the present dogmas being essentially fleetingly true and fleetingly valuable, let us conceive a set 'A' within which "honesty" is "good" (or valuable) and it is absolutely true within that set at a particular time but it may well be that within that set 'A' in another time, "honesty" is "bad", is also absolutely true. The conclusion is that, in itself, 'honesty' is value-neutral. It is a mere phenomenon evaluated within a set 'A' at different times, differently. Then we have to assume that at time, t_1 there is perfect agreement among participants within set 'A' about the value of "honesty" and so is the case at time t_2, but the value has changed drastically. There are two questions. Is it possible within the relativistic system to have a perfect moral agreement about values? The answer is yes, if the set is too small and no, if the set is large. In societies, we do conceive both sets and we have to accept both answers to be true. The next question is, why does the value system of set A change from time t_1 to t_2 regarding "honesty", if there is a perfect agreement? To save us, we have to say now that whatever small the set is, there is every chance of disagreement or that all social sets have disagreement tendencies about values, and therefore, our entire value-system is relative. We have thus agreed to the thesis that within any social set at any time, there is a constant flux of ethical agreement and disagreement and no perfect agreement or perfect disagreement is conceivable. Then how to do we assume that "honesty is good" is an evaluation, which reflects the whole ethic of a group or a set even at a point of time? In addition, how do we assume that "honesty is bad now" means, it is the reflection of the whole group-ethic now? Ethical relativism tends to be highly subjectivist if it shuns its original position that what an individual asserts about "honesty" is true to the entire group. In fact, if within a group, the individualistic relativism about values is pressed too far then there can be no social, as well as racial ethical dogmas. There may be individual ethical dogmas only, each tending to be true. Now if individual dogmas are all true, and ethics is just this then, what could be generalized as a standard is not known to us, and if we do not have a standard other than the standard that "all individual ethical values are true whatever may be the changing place and time", do we really have standard at all? The generalization principles in ethics cannot be the one like, "all social dogmas are true" and "all individual dogmas are true". This is dangerous because within Czarist regime if mass killing was good then it was good at the time. What about individual relativism at that time? A man during Czarist Russia may be the one who did not agree to this fact, and then he too is correct in his way of thinking. Again, after the Revolution, if dictatorship of the proletariat was "good" then what about the one who did not believe so? Was he correct as well? More pressing question will be why is it that suddenly after the revolution, "the dictatorship of the proletariat" turned out to be "the good" and "mass killing of Czars", "the bad"? What is the criterion? It cannot be the dull relativism and subjectivism because we fall in trap of accepting the goodness of both. We have maintained that one turns out to be "really good" or "generally desirable" for all times to come, may be we have the standard of "welfarism". However, this is a very different general ethical standard, not supporting ethical relativism. However, ethical relativism has a half-truth hidden for us, i.e., general ethical standards are many and not one and our evaluations are relative according to the relative choice of ethical standards. However, the choice every time is our choice, so that individual's free will has its known place as well. So ethics is not merely, "what I think or I value to be good" and not "what we think or we value to be good". It is due to this that "honesty" can be evaluated both as "good" and as "bad" depending on different moral criterion or on the choice of different moral standards by us. Here is the half-truth of ethical relativism.

From this, we also come to know that ethics is not mere personal exhortations of emotions towards some human actions and decisions as thinks some emotivists. No doubt, the emotivists do care for the basic truth that ethical exhortations are emotional in nature because the speaker expresses his or her agreement and disagreement through these exhortations. They reflect their attitude so to say. Nevertheless, this is not the whole story because ethical evaluations or evaluative exhortations are something more. They may be suggestive and prescriptive exhortations as well. Moreover, we must not forget that when we express our approbative emotions by saying, "honesty is good", we may still ask about the basis of such approbation and the basis cannot be our whims or subjective predilections. Because a subjective orientation would end up in queer relativism, where all will turn out to be true and it will be difficult to find out the reasons behind expressing such and such emotions towards such and such things. To borrow the idea of Nowell-Smith, ethical exhortations may be "Janus headed"[1] and therefore, cannot be merely emotive in nature. What we get is that ethics is not about expressions of personal predilections regarding human actions and decisions. We also need not forget that ethics is not merely irrational or non-rational expressions of emotions towards human actions and decisions. The role of reason and rational basis of emotive exhortations can never be ruled out from ethics. Similarly, when we accept an ethical general standard, we can never rule out the role of rational justification and rational arguments.

If we have accepted at least obliquely that emotions, approbations, disagreements, suggestions etc. are closely related to the meaningfulness of ethical exhortations, we have accepted the truth that some way or other ethics has an affinity with psychic sphere of the moral doer and moral evaluator. This becomes far clearer when we speak elaborately about the psychological basis of ethics, particularly, when we deal with motives, inclinations, attitudes, beliefs, desires, pleasures and so on. Many people have an idea that ethics is all psychology, which, it is not. For one thing, not all ethical assertions can be transmuted to psychological assertions, and, therefore, ethical language cannot be wholly analyzed for its meaning on psychological grounds. There will be clear category confusion if we tend to attempt at replacing one with the other on the fictitious ground that ethics does have a descriptive part and the part is mainly psychological. Let us make it clearer. Ethics, for instance, may speak about emotions of speakers being expressed through ethical judgments like "Honesty is good". This is to say, "I approve of honesty so you do so as well". However, ethics would not consider delving deeper into questions like, 'what are emotions? What are its causes? What are its kinds? What are the causes of ethical emotions? What goes on in one's mind when one expresses an emotion like the one above?' These questions are in fact psychological questions with which ethics has nothing to do. However, an ethical thinker, who knows nothing about 'emotions' would never propose an emotive explanation of ethical meaningfulness but that does not prove that therefore ethicists are performing the task of psychologists. A psychologist would propose clear psychophysical description of the above questions and may have nothing to do with 'ethical emotions' but that does not prevent a psychologist to discuss about 'ethical emotions'. Only thing is he or she would not take up the case of ethical emotions in the way ethicists do, i.e., to provide an explanation of meaning of ethical assertions. Hence, ethicists' interest in 'emotion' and the psychologists' interest in the same thing are not similar. We do find a lot of discussion in ethics about 'pleasure' and 'happiness' and also about 'feelings', 'sensations' etc. It is not that ethicists talking about 'pleasure as desirable' does not know the psychological explanation of 'pleasure', 'desire', 'feelings' and so on, rather they should know such things. Nevertheless, the psychological descriptions provide only a basis to ethically oriented discussion because as we see here, we have considered pleasure not merely as a 'desire' but the sense in which it is 'desirable' or 'worth having' or simply 'good'. An ethicist may not be interested therefore to know the details and nuances of 'feeling theories' or 'desire explanations' or in particular, 'what happens in our minds when we have desires of pleasure'. These are in fact psychological inquiries. Therefore, ethics is not all psychology.

There is a final confusion in the minds of both philosophers and non-philosophers, i.e., ethics is an art of teaching how social life has to be lived and that it lays principles of converting evil souls to noble ones. Ethics is thus an art of dignified living. Let us clarify that ethics first is not an art, like the art of painting or music and thus not an art of living a good life. One may wonder now. You said that it does discuss about goodness, about standards of moral evaluation and so on but now you say, it has nothing to do with a good life. Then ethics must be all good to read and no good to follow. It is in fact impractical theoretical jugglery. Those, who think that ethics takes the burden to teach the art of ethical living, should know that it is very difficult nay absurd to teach this art. What is this art after all? When is living ethical? In addition, if it is an art, what are the methods and rules, which ought to be taught for an artful ethical life? The problem is, we can hardly tell clearly about the art of ethics as we can easily explain the art of music because the art of music consists of a set of rules, which are taught for a musical performance, and with practice, we can hone up the skill more and more. However, there are no definite rules or set of rules of ethics, which can be taught to people followed by regular practice to hone up their skill of becoming perfectly ethical people. One may wonder, why not! We do have codes and rules in ethics, which have been taught since a long time by our family, teachers, religious *gurus* and so on. Did we even ponder about these codes and rules? These codes and rules are like commands, prescriptions of do's and don'ts given by elders and revered people, which are believed to be helpful for leading a good life. However, we have seen in our earlier discussion that these rules are mere means or cues following first principles of morality. For instance, if the basic standard of morality for someone is, "providing happiness to maximum people", a code follows, "help the poor and needy". Now if you fix up this code "help the poor" to be taught to your pupils wanting to live a good life, you may easily do that not leaving of course the basic teaching, "that in doing so you will attain 'general welfare' as the ultimate good". Similarly, we can go for a number of such teachings and we expect our good pupils follow them to hone up their art of living ethically. Plato taught another story in his Republic. He said, sometimes our good pupils may suddenly discover that "helping poor" and "telling truth" turns out to be extremely unethical and at times foolish. So do we now teach ourselves another rule of artful life, viz., "tell a lie at times" and "do not help the poor always"? Try them, you will find that you have been put to another foolish trial and error. Therefore, there can be no set of rules taught for ethical living unless the meaning of "ethical" is clear to our pupils. For this knowledge, however one has to come to theoretical ethics and there is no need to attend the classes of ethics *gurus* or other *gurus* who are at best the modern incarnations of arts, the Sophists. There is no sophistry in ethics because ethics does not teach us to live ethically by means of certain rules. It is almost like logic. You cannot teach the rules of logic to your students to talk or argue logically because there is no art of logic. This does not mean that ethics is a theoretical jugglery and impractical for life. To know about the practicability of ethics, we have to know its third task, the application of ethics but we shall not discuss it now. Yet, one should know that even application of ethics does not amount to the teaching of the first principles of morality for their efficient application in daily life. It is something else. We should remember that ethical teachings of great *gurus* have been only relatively valuable, they are highly debatable, justifiable and liable to be rejected with changing time. There is no point in either teaching them or blindly following them. We must also remember that by teaching ethical codes or through reading academic ethics, one can never convert his or her 'not so noble character' into a 'noble one' or can convert any wicked soul to a noble one. In fact, academic ethics in anyway does not assume the hopeless burden of sophistry, which is commonly heaped on ethics (tragically). This is due to the simple reason that perhaps we have no perfect ethical souls nor perfectly unethical souls as we do not have a perfect straight or curved line. Because we often decide at a particular point of time souls become wicked and noble, which however is often disagreed by others. Therefore, it is better not to try to do all these things. We are perhaps, as Plato says, possessors of 'capacity of opposites' (Dr. Jekyll and Mr. Hyde type), and our capacities are often displayed in the public. Therefore, the public or I may judge them easily following moral standards. So why bother about converting others and yourself in the completely artificial and absurd way of teaching ethical rules of living? Therefore, ethics is not an art, i.e., an art of good living. Again the nagging question (we raised before) may be raised, 'has ethics nothing to do with value based decision making in practical life?' Can we not formulate some such rules of decision making which may turn out to be aid to a vibrant ethical life of the society? We shall take up these questions at an appropriate place.

Now we have to come to face an anti-climax, i.e., to know clearly what ethics is. (It is perhaps clear to the readers by this time). Clearly, ethics is a branch of philosophy, the definition of which is a little cumbersome because it amounts to nothing but statement of the tasks of ethics and with it, the branches of ethics. Therefore, we should better state what the tasks of ethics are. First, ethics is philosophical thinking about questions pertaining to morality, moral problems and moral language. G.E. Moore says that one, who does not have a clear idea about moral language in use, perhaps does not know the crux of ethics. Truly, if one does not have a clear idea about what is "good", "bad", "right", "wrong", "duty", "obligation" etc. one is not in a position to tell us anything about moral assertions and moral judgments because these are some of the fundamental moral concepts, the meaning of which should be clarified. Moreover, what are moral or evaluative judgments? How are they different from other judgments? The problem is what is judged and what is the proper object of such judgment? These are some of the interesting moral problems. Nevertheless, these problems transcend normative discussions because they are problems about language. We call them "metaethical problems" considered within "metaethics". Apart from this when we speak about moral standards in our normative discussion, we speak about the justification of such standards, which is again a metaethical discussion because it takes us to the logical basis of ethical evaluation.

The normative part of ethical thinking within which we consider the problem of moral evaluation or evaluation of intended human actions, considers the problem of laying standards of moral evaluation. We have seen that there are many ethical criteria for deciding the rightness, the goodness, the desirableness of intended human actions. The discussion is often contextual as far as we are considering particular intended act and attempt to decide about its rightness and goodness (given the standards) and then construct normative judgments. Or else the discussion may be more general as far as we are considering some moral traits or virtues like "honesty" and decide upon their moral worth given the norms of morality. It is here, therefore, that debates about moral judgment need an explicit statement of moral standards and their justification.

More recently many ethicists are limiting the tasks of ethics to the normative and the metaethical, and some have been more radical to call it purely analytic or metaethical. However, this is to forget that ethics has another important task, the "applied task". It is here we may turn to our question about decision-making rules in ethics. The question is, if ethics is not framing fixed set of rules, particularly like commandments or the do's and don'ts because that hardly helps us in becoming moral, why do some of us in ethics still speak about practical decision making rules? To answer this question appropriately, we have to know what is applying ethics and why one of the fruits of applying ethics is to formulate ethical decision-making rules for our professionals. Again, if we understand this, we will be able to understand what are the pragmatic or the practical values of the subject called ethics. This may enable us to shrug off the old fashioned idea that ethics is good to read but not good in practice. This may further enable us to know why ethics never aim at making us moral or noble but it still has a definite applied or practical task to perform. Hence, we should know about this new passion called "applying ethics". It is relatively new because whatever may be its past heritage, we did not discuss it separately and prominently before the Vietnam War. However, it has now become an ardent passion among the ethicists; thanks to the epidemic publish or perish syndrome among the intellectuals. The ardent supporters of applied ethics now believe that ethicists may consider another interdisciplinary task to resolve value-laden practical problem troubling the professionals in different fields. They believe that in doing so our professionals may be provided with ethical acumen to face moral impasse in practical life more effectively. However, how this has to be done, is the key to the problem. There is a great debate about what consists of application of ethics.

Most interesting fact is that even today many ethicists are skeptical about this task of ethics. Moreover, I have said that many are skeptical about the normative task as well. Therefore, we have to go through the arguments of those ethicists who have serious doubts about normative ethics and applied ethics and try to counter-argue to show that the whole body of ethics consists of at least three tasks—the metaethical, the normative and applied and that they are within ethics. In reality, all three tasks of ethics or the branches of ethics are closely interwoven. If we fail to understand this, it is pointless discussing the details of applied ethics. So let us move on to explore the three inter-related tasks of ethics.

We have made considerable progress in the field of ethics. However, even today, there are philosophers who do not agree that normative ethics and practical ethics are within the broad field of ethics. The sharpest disagreement is about applied ethics. My responsibility is to show that normative ethics, metaethics and applied ethics are all included within what we call "ethics" because neglecting one is to encourage an ethics, which is not 'ethics proper'. It may be argued that neglecting applied ethics in particular, is to encourage a moral philosophy, which is not moral. At the outset, it is very important to explain what normative ethics and metaethics consists in, and why they are intimately related in the broad field of ethics.

Normative ethics or substantive ethics attempts at answering the fundamental questions in morality, i.e. what is good or right in particular case and what is the basis of judging something as good and right. Hence, normative ethics mainly deals with the basic principles or standards of morality, about their nature, about the secondary moral rules that follow from them and the way such standards are helpful in judging the morality of intentional human actions. Normative ethics thus supplies grounds for moral evaluation. It also deals with questions about our rights, duties, obligations etc.

Metaethics, on the other hand, deals with logical and semantic questions like, what are the meanings and uses of moral terms (good, right etc.) and moral judgments ('X is good' etc.) What justifications or proofs can we give in favour of a moral principle? How are ethical evaluations justified? What do we mean by "freedom" and "determinism"? etc. It is very important to discuss metaethical questions in ethics, because metaethics encourages analytical and critical thinking about moral language and moral evaluation. However, to call metaethics ethics proper is too trite. There is no doubt, however, that there are many moral thinkers who believe that the task of ethics proper is to engage in metaethical questions. This amounts to the growth of 'exclusive metaethics' by neglecting normative and applied ethics completely. We have to face such neglect towards the important branches of ethics because not all of us may like the idea that ethics has a factual anchor. Nevertheless, to face this challenge we have to know where the challenge comes from and what the reasons behind such challenge are.

The early positivists were extreme skeptics who hold that the whole gamut of ethical discourse is as meaningless and as nonsensical as are the religious and metaphysical discourses. This is so because one type of ethical propositions is descriptive statements about ethical situations and responses, which statements belong to the empirical science of psychology and not ethics at all. The other type consists of the normative statements, which belong to ethics, but is as nonsensical and meaningless as metaphysical statements because these assertions have no empirical basis and are thus unverifiable.[2] If normative statements turn out to be nonsensical and meaningless, there can be no moral standards as well and all discussions of moral merit, freedom or responsibility lose significance. Naturally, if we cannot sensibly speak of moral standards, it is useless to think about moral evaluations as well. In fact, "good", "bad", "evil" etc. is not evaluative words in the sense that we normally think them to be. They are rather words expressing our emotions. We may thus say that the natural outcome of extreme positivism has been the complete rejection of normative ethics. However, the effort was so self-defeating that with the death of normative ethics, the possibility of ethics was nearly put in the grave, until softer versions adopted a new course in ethical discussion. This is emotivism. It still doubted factual validity of ethical statements and raised questions about the validity of ethical standards and their justification. The standards are at best emotive expressions of a person with regard to the ideals of life and the basis of ethical judgments. The softer version of ethical skepticism was mainly supported by people like Ayer who did not think that the entire gamut of ethical language could be put into oblivion rather; they may be non-cognitively meaningful as they are the expressions of the emotion of those who use this language. Ayer says, "in so far as statements of value are significant ... They are simply expressions of emotions which can be neither true nor false."[3] With this, Ayer also paved the way for "exclusive metaethics" in confining the task of moral philosophy to the study of ethical language and nothing else. This is in perfect consonance with another commitment of the positivists that 'philosophy is the logical analysis of language'. Hence, the positivists' and the analysts' claim that the task of ethics can be nothing more than the 'analysis of ethical language' paved way for rejecting normative ethics and applied ethics. Ayer says that ethics consists of "propositions which express definitions of ethical terms, or judgments about the legitimacy or possibility of certain definitions"[4]. However, the natural outcome of such a line of thinking is to forget that the proving and justification of ethical theories are also interesting metaethical issues in ethics. The emotivists need to reject this as well, for ethical theories being no theories at all, are reduced to a bundle of emotive expressions. As such, ethical theories cannot be accepted as the basis of the evaluation of human actions. There is thus no need for having any standards in morality and no need to prove or justify them. With this, they accept that there are not moral or evaluative terms or concepts in the real sense of the term because these are "pseudo-concepts".[5] Hence, these terms serve no purpose other than to express emotions of the speaker who uses them in ethical language. "Good" is thus not an ethical concept or evaluative term at all, and evaluating actions, is no business of the philosophers. However, we may go on analyzing ethical language *qua* philosophers.

The emotivists were, however, a divided lot by the time C.L. Stevenson forcefully joined the foray of ethical skepticism. He was not as drastic as declaring that being emotive in nature, ethical language serves no useful purpose. Stevenson was of the opinion that apart from reflecting the emotions, ethical language contains such notions as "good" and "bad" which also evokes either ethical agreement or disagreement. Not only this, he finds in these words and in ethical judgments, the element of "persuasiveness". Persuasive language has many uses and ethical language as such cannot be ignored as serving no useful purpose. Stevenson says, "It is certainly mandatory that the term "emotive" be kept as a tool for use in careful study not as a device for relegating the non-descriptive aspects of language to the limbo".[6] With this, Stevenson also moves a step beyond extreme skepticism in order to recognize in ethical judgments the place of descriptive element and has gone a long way towards acknowledging a validity in ethics which seems to be first denied by linguistic analysts. However, there is no doubt that the skeptics have no place for normative and applied questions in ethics in their scheme. We find this with Schlick's clear admittance of the fact that "the moral valuations of moral behaviour are nothing but the emotional reactions with which the human society responds to the pleasant and sorrowful consequences..."[7] Astonishingly Schlick was not too far from developing an ethical theory himself by holding that "in human society, that is called good which is believed to bring the greatest happiness".[8]

Given this background of discarding substantive ethical questions from ethics proper and confining ethics to 'exclusive metaethics', we have to prove a negative point, that is, this is not 'ethics properly so called'. The extreme positivists and the emotivists based their arguments on the fact that moral judgments do not attribute some intelligible characteristics or relation to the objects or actions, which they judge, and in denying this these thinkers express unilateral view regarding moral experience. However, they fail to see one very important aspect of 'moral experience'; that is, we have enough empirical basis to show that moral terms, in fact, become descriptively meaningful in the real contexts of their uses in moral language. Again, we have enough empirical ground to show that moral standards become descriptively meaningful as well. These thinkers also forget that as far as the moral experience is concerned, moral judgments present themselves in these experiences as well as reasoned judgments. However, by saying that moral judgments are only emotive judgments, they miss an important point. If moral judgments are essentially emotive in nature and have neither empirical anchor nor any reason behind it, it is doomed to be equally true and false, and as such, it will be difficult even to make any moral distinction, with the help of these judgments. If this were true then the search for moral worth turns out be a hopeless venture, it will be equally hopeless to search for moral truth. All these blunders committed by the extreme positivists and emotivists compel us to say that they did not even understand the basic truth that they are conceiving of an ethics which is entirely based non-empirically and they take up the task of linguistic analysis of ethical language, which is completely in variance with moral experience and ordinary linguistic usage.

No doubt, Schlick and Stevenson brushed off extreme positivists' orthodoxy and recognized that moral judgments are at least based upon and in part verifiable by factual judgments. They also recognized the truth that ethical language may have more functions than one, and therefore, approbative and persuasive functions were discussed. Nevertheless, they were still lurking in the realm of 'exclusive metaethics' by holding that establishing moral theories is needless. The basic prejudice that haunts their minds may he that we can speak of only one proper function of ethics, as is the case with philosophy. The proper function is the "logical analysis of language". Hence, the peculiar self-made division of labour still compels the later emotivists to believe that ethical theories and their justification are needless. If we consider logic itself as a branch of philosophy, it is not philosophical analysis of language, rather provides the basis of such analysis. Hence, philosophy as a branch of knowledge cannot be the only logical analysis of language, ethics also cannot be the only analysis of ethical language because the language of ethics is a testimony to the fact that apart from serving many functions, it also serves to evaluate the worth or value of intentional human actions. We have enough empirical ground to claim this. The evaluative function presupposes ethical standards as well. Hence, it is perfectly legitimate to say that normative ethics is within ethics.

We will also have to understand that to speak of these standards is vacuous if we do not conceive of the disposition of these theories to resolve value-laden problems. However, in ethics we may speak of the primacy of functions as a matter of strategy. The strategies of Plato and Moore were to move from metaethical questions to the construction of an ethical theory (which is a normative ethical discourse). Whereas, Mill's strategy is different, he starts with the explanation of a standard and then moves on to the metaethical task of the justification of the standard of morality. Hence, the strategic primacy of metaethics is not to say that ethics is just metaethics. The same is true in case of normative ethics. It is needless arguing that there is a first order task in ethics or that ethics is what constitutes its first order task. All the normative, metaethical and applied ethical tasks are of equal importance in ethics. Hence, exclusive metaethics is to encourage an ethics that forgets this basic truth that there is more than one function of ethics. As such, 'exclusive metaethics' is not "ethics properly so called". However to prove this positive point that normative ethics and metaethics are closely related and not only within ethics, we have to consider ethical judgments, not in isolation, rather in relation to the need for passing such judgments, the functions or uses of these judgments, the actual act of judgments in a real life situation and the basis of passing such judgments.

Let us consider an ethical judgment (the sense in which an emotivist understands it and finds it to be meaningful). Suppose I say, "Telling truth is good". The emotivists hold that this judgment may be meaningful only in relation to the one who is using such assertion to express either his emotions towards "truth telling" or he aims at persuading others that they also "tell truth" because they approve of it as good and others ought to do so as well. One thing is clear by now, the moral term "good" in this context of its use may be meaningful in more sense than one. Another thing is that the moral term "good" is not simply a term in the sense that it has been taken from the vast repository of English language rather; it is a term, which is used distinctly to evaluate intentional human actions and is thus an evaluative term or a value term. No doubt in moral evaluation of actions (e.g., truth telling), the emotions, feelings, approbation, agreement, disagreement etc. are all very important (interestingly, even this can be known in a real life situation with the aid of actual experience and not by *a priori* thinking). However, to say that this is all is to forget that this moral judgment is not only persuasive and prescriptive in nature, but evaluative as well. Hence, moral terms are also evaluative terms and moral judgments are evaluative judgments. There is no need at all to lose sight of the evaluative function of these terms and judgments because recognition of this truth is in no way detrimental to what emotivist uphold. It is in fact an important aid to a proper understanding of the nature and function of ethical terms and ethical judgments. Moral judgments are in fact not only expressive of emotions; they are so about the value of actions or about the worth of actions.

There may be no doubt however that a non-philosopher is well aware of the fact that he is expressing his emotion towards "truth telling" and that he may be approving it, persuading others and may even prescribe it for other to do so. Nevertheless, does a "non-philosopher" have the knowledge that he is in fact evaluating a moral action and for that reason, he ought to presume a moral standard? Any sane, social person, who lives an active moral life, mixes with "moral agents" influences others with his intentional actions and is also influenced by the actions of other people, has varied moral experience which is an aid to moral knowledge. It is a "stark truth" that while judging "truth telling" as "good" one is in fact judging action as having moral worth, one is sure that what he is evaluating is not a thing. He is also aware that while he is evaluating, he has enough reasons for doing so. This latter knowledge takes us to the specified theoretical consideration of the standards of evaluation. Hence, the knowledge of the fact that for moral evaluation we have to take recourse to a moral standard as well is also not possible without social interaction and moral experience obtained thereby. Readers may be worried about the fact that I have assumed many things *qua* philosopher and have not put myself in place of a non-philosopher. The 'stark truth' I was speaking about is not a matter of either intuition or pure reason; it is a matter of experience, which, I shall consider at a proper place. For the moment, it is sufficient to say that the knowledge of moral evaluation is impossible if we do not have an actual urge for evaluating the worth of an action. This urge is moral urge that a social being feels, for he participates in active moral discourse and active moral life in the society. If we are bereft of such urge and do not have an inclination for moral interaction with other beings, we are devoid of moral experience and are thus in a hopeless state of knowledge. It is then we feel that 'good', 'bad', 'right', 'wrong' are mere terms, waiting there to express our emotions and nothing else. However, they have many things to do, is what is most important to know. In fact, moral experience is so crucial and unavoidable that it hardly makes any sense to distinguish a philosopher from a non-philosopher because of the need for such an experience in moral life.

Nevertheless, a philosopher, who has a professional training in ethics, may come to realize that there may not be only one standard of moral evaluation. He may look into the soundness of the logic behind accepting a theory to be worthy of judging moral actions. However, even an ethicist cannot overlook that the moral experience that are made possible by social interaction are unavoidable. Once we understand this, we come to know that if one task of ethics is the analysis of ethical language, the other task is to enquire about the basis of moral evaluation. As such, metaethical and normative enquiries are both important and closely related. An ethical enquiry certainly leads to five things: (a) moral evaluation of intentional actions, (b) conceiving the basis of moral evaluation, (c) the soundness of the logic of accepting ethical standards worth judging the morality of actions, (d) the nature and function of ethical terms and ethical judgments, and (e) the application of ethical experience and ethics knowledge to resolve moral crisis. The (c) and (d) are included in metaethics, whereas the (a) and (b) are included in normative ethics. It is needless to argue too much about the fact that (a), (b) and (d) clearly state that metaethical and normative ethical enquiries are closely related in ethics proper. However, we cannot overlook (e) as well. We shall have to justify this elaborately.

Yes, there may be serious concern about the significance of moral experience itself because such an experience may lead us to the gross acceptance of social norms and customs as the basis of moral evaluation. If this were the case then another skeptical line of thought comes into the limelight. This speaks of the fact that there are no moral standards and moral evaluations at all because what is there is the mere acceptance of social norms and customs, which cannot become a standard, for they are intrinsically changeable and are thus relative. They cannot be the basis of the moral evaluation." Again, one may think that experience of social customs cannot help us in establishing a general moral theory because moral agent transcends all experience to take recourse to intuitive subsumption while he is involved in ethical generalization. Let us consider at the face value of individuals' capacity to frame a moral theory with the help of either pure reason or intuition. These may be appalling possibilities in justification of ethical principles. Hence, we may believe that it is intuition and not experience which is crucial in morality. We must not forget that devoid of an active social life and incessant moral experience, a sane person will not even feel an urgency to think of a moral standard of evaluation, what to speak of justifying it. In fact, the empirical basis of morality is the starting point in morality. Morality needs the help of reasoning but without actual moral experience nothing can proceed. No rational insight about moral standards and no *a priori* conception of values and standards can help us in morality unless we conceive of homosapiens living here in this world, having intricate relationship with the entire ecological community, acting, influencing, judging and evaluating. We cannot thus speak of a sensible moral philosophy without moral experience. However, this does not imply that we follow such rules and customs in moral evaluations. Having experience in the society and following social rules and customs are two different things. We may have constant moral experience in the society but we may not follow a particular social rule and custom. We may like to change them or revolt against them or like to correct them. In fact, our ideas about moral standards and about their legitimacy in moral thinking are not with fixed social customs. Tragically if someone thinks it to be pertinent enough to follow social rules in morality, he may be rightly following a set of relatively useful rules for himself and may not necessarily generalize it as a standard of morality for all times to come and for all societies. The need for a generalized ethical principle other than the social rules may be helpful for us. Such general ethical principles ignore the change of time. That this is possible is again a matter of experience. Active moral life in a society and experience obtained therein are the prerequisites of holistic ethical knowledge and a knowledge that combines metaethics, normative ethics and applied ethics. Let us now finally bring closer the linguistic, extra-linguistic and the practical aspects of human life because this is the cornerstone of moving towards an understanding of applied ethics. However, before that another point has to be made clear.

Semantic considerations in moral philosophy consist in language distinctions, which is not beyond the reach of the non-philosophers. We also have to understand that the language of moral philosophy is used also for analyzing aspects of human life, which are not mere language distinction, and mere emotive exhortations of those who use moral language for practical purpose. Languages are one aspect of human life and morality is another one. Both language and morality are related as far as language is used for moral distinctions, expressive of moral feelings, emotions, and sentiments and for the clarification of the moral points of views. Nevertheless, what is of utmost importance is to understand that moral language (including moral terms used therein), is instrumental in referring to the "concrete demands in action" with which a person is confronted in his social relation.[9] The "concrete demands" are facts, which we must consider seriously in moral philosophy. There is no doubt that the term "good" may be considered apart from moral considerations; however, in so far as it is used in moral evaluation, we cannot avoid the manifold "concrete demands in action" with which a person is confronted in social contexts. The terms like "good" are, of course, partly useful in expressing emotions of an evaluator. That they are useful in prescribing a course of action is also true. However, not every evaluative term in the vocabulary of moral philosophy is devoid of factual significance. This is so because these terms in an intelligently thought-out moral philosophy are "factual" when they refer to aspect of human life or refer to "facts" in the context in which men live. Ben Kimpel brings out the truth elegantly by saying that, "the terms 'right' and 'good' for instance, refer to realities, which are 'factual'… The realities referred to in moral philosophies are not, of course, the realities, which are studied in some of the specialized sciences. But this fact constitutes no disparagement of the vocabulary of moral philosophy".[10] We should understand, therefore, that in case of the distinctions of moral worth, we refer not only to language distinctions and to other conventional distinctions, but also to human life. Now as we consider the very basis of the moral distinction or distinctions of moral worth, we certainly have to consider human experiences and social interactions into considerations. The confusion that the very basis of moral evaluation is devoid of an empirical consideration ought to be dispelled. Once we do this, we will come to know that ethical first principles are neither purely emotive exhortations nor mere *a priori* constructions of our mind. We have just seen that an evaluative judgment like, "truth telling is good" implies that "truth telling" is something, which is "morally good". This has any meaning at all if "truth telling" is a moral action which is sensible to speak about and it is sensible to speak about its moral worth. We are also concerned about whether or not it really contributes to the moral quality of human life. Whether or not an intentional human action like this is at all contributing to the moral quality of human life is a matter of empirical enquiry again. I would like to remind here that some intentional human actions might not be contributing to human life in the real sense if they overlook the quality of the life of the entire ecological community as well. Whatever, it may be, it is very clear that the goodness or moral worth of actions like "truth telling" can be evaluated as such in the context of a generalized principle of morality of keeping in view of generalized principal of morality or keeping in view a moral ideal. A possibility of such moral basis leads us to construct a moral theory. Moral ideals thus speak of intrinsic worth which are desirable in life and which are the basis of the evaluation of moral actions. It is interesting to notice that the conception of a moral theory may not be groundless. Rather, it has to be justified. Most of the time we think that the justification can be something devoid of experience because moral principles are not experienced; they are either logically proved or intuited generalizations. I have already remarked how baseless it is to speak of intuiting a moral principle without actual experiences in terms of social and human interactions, it is also useless to have an intuited principle and not to think that it is desirable and worth contributing to the quality of human life.

We also know that the establishment of moral principles based on strict deductive and inductive rules is fraught with a danger. We may, however, speak of not proving but informally justifying such principles. In that case, informal justification is not merely subjective whim or psychological in character; it may not be according to strict rules of logic but may be logical. Whatever it may be, it still has a strong empirical anchor because the instances of human interactions in the real life situation may be strong grounds for informal justification of a generalized ethical principle. Hence, even if we leave out strict deductive and inductive proofs in the establishment of ethical principles, either informal justification or logical justification or even intuitive subsumption is not devoid of an empirical consideration. The obvious reason is that moral ideals, their conception, justification and desirability make any sense at all if we do not lose sight of the life of the homosapiens and their interactions with other members of the ecological community. No moral theory can be even conceived of without this basic empirical consideration. Now that we have made enough advances in the field of ethics, we will not be ready to consider divine standard as a serious possibility, yet, if we reflect on the nature of it, and think that it has any value at all, it has to be seen whether or not in the real life situation it has any relation with the quality of life of the homosapiens. I would thus like to add that deontology or teleology or divine standard, a moral theory is moral if it contributes to the quality of human life in the real sense. In addition, for this, we ought to consider the factual aspects of human life. The readers ought to be careful here to notice that what I mean to say has nothing to do with the justification of any one moral theory I am trying to bring about the basic truth of a moral philosophy, which is moral. I must also remind the reader that it is now that we must realize how important it is to consider together the questions of normative ethics (about a moral ideal) and the questions of metaethics (about justification of moral principles and linguistic concerns in evaluations). Both these are inseparable and equally important parts of ethics.

I believe that we have by now become equally concerned with the 'quality of the human life' and the 'real life situations' in considering in detail the fundamentals of a moral philosophy having a moral worth. One who really does not lose sight of these things can easily understand that ethics is just not normative ethics and metaethics; it is something more. We thus arrive at understanding the fact that applied ethics or practical ethics is within ethics and to neglect it is to neglect holistic ethics, which includes an understanding of applied ethics as well. It is now that we must know what applied ethics really is and why it is different from application of ethical codes, maxims and commands. Applied ethics involves in considering one or more value-laden problems in the society in which we live to find out how they may be resolved and what set of practical decision-making rules ought to be framed having a moral face. In other words, applied ethics consists in formulating practical decision-making rules (having not only practical value but moral value as well) in the face of resolution of value-laden problems in an emphatic manner. Nowhere did I say that such value-laden problems are supplied by non-philosophers. No one supplies value-laden problems; value-laden problems are there, evolving, growing, changing, and fizzling out in our societies. They are to be identified by us to resolve them. I have also not said that philosophers having knowledge of ethical theories act as moral saviours to resolve moral crisis by pressing into service any one or more ethical theory or theories. This is as nonsensical as the earlier belief. A value-laden problem in fact cannot be resolved emphatically and practical decision making rules having moral value cannot be framed by a philosopher alone, it needs corroboration or moral viewpoints. I have been laying stress on the fact that every social being has moral experience and optimum moral knowledge. As such, every person may have a moral viewpoint regarding any ethical dilemma. Philosophers might have specialized knowledge of ethical theories in addition to the moral experience and moral knowledge that everybody has. This may be extremely helpful in coming to consensus in framing practical rules and resolving value-laden problems. Once we are involved in a cooperative venture like this one, we are involved in applying ethics. The role of the philosopher may be unique. He may encourage moral discussion, he may point out the moral hunches a person has, he may point out the nuances between the moral point of view and their relative advantages and disadvantages in resolving a moral impasse, he may try to smother moral disagreement and most importantly, he may help in reaching a moral consensus to frame practical decision making rules having moral value. A philosopher is thus just one important party in applying ethics. But he needs others as well because without other parties, there may not be any corroboration of moral views, we may not know how different people would like to resolve a moral problem and what moral theory or theories figure out prominently in resolving a value-laden problem and in framing practical rules in the society. In an applied ethical venture, a philosopher is not an ethical vanguard, he is an ethical corroborator. Further, we may see that the philosophers and the non-philosophers need not engineer normative principles in an artificial, mechanical manner. To face a moral crisis, corroboration of moral view points, reaching a consensus, solving a problem and framing rules does not presuppose moral engineers (the philosophers in particular). Hence, applying ethical theories need not mean moral engineering by ethics experts. Nevertheless, the philosophers have a unique role to play in this regard. He may reflect on ethical corroboration and the outcome of such corroboration to discover the way one more ethical theory have been helpful in resolving a moral crisis and in framing practical rules. This is the application of the specialized ethical knowledge of a philosopher to know and let people know about the practical or applied value of a normative principle. This is a purely theoretical venture, which may be done in perfect isolation, having informative and educative value in the society. This posterior theoretical effort of a philosopher is one aspect of applied ethics, which has academic value. It may well be that in the end, in democratic societies, where applying ethics has become a continuous process and a social creed; it may contribute to the growth of the moral knowledge of all concerned people. If this happens, applying ethical knowledge has a sounder basis, and in the course of ethical corroboration to resolve moral crisis, it is sure to play a vital role about which we may not be conscious. In fact, ethical theories (normative) are not to be applied just as tool in a toolbox is used to mend something. In applied or practical ethics venture, we do not apply an ethical theory like that; we may corroborate ethical viewpoints and then discover what ethical theory has been most fruitful in resolving a moral problem. In addition, as I have said, if this becomes a national creed, people may be informed about these theories. In an applied ethical venture, we may find to our astonishment how wonderfully all of us participate in ethical discourses in which ethical theories reflect themselves lest ethicists have the urge to analyze. Let us think rationally. The construction and justification of normative ethical theories are the historical facts but that they are potent enough in solving moral crises is a matter of discovery when we are involved in ethical corroboration. It is then we come to know and let others know about such intrinsic practical value of a moral theory. Hence in applying ethics: (a) a value-laden problem has to be identified; (b) corroboration of moral view points in resolving the value-laden problems has to be initiated by a philosopher; (c) moral consensus has to be reached in order to frame practical rules in resolving a moral problem; and (d) philosophers may then analyze the whole discourse to discover the way that one ethical theory or many ethical theories have been useful in framing practical rules in society and thus in resolving moral problems. It is clear that applying ethics is not applying any one theory by a philosopher. However, whether or not theories are practically useful, is not a matter of academic inquiry.

One may wonder given this sense of applying ethics, can we really apply ethical theories! We must be careful that the sense in which I have considered applying ethics to be is not only "applying ethical theories by an ethics expert". There is no point in thinking that 'applied ethics' is philosophers applying ethical theories; (If we fall in this trap, we start thinking that applied ethics is ethicists' business and ethical theories are used as tool in toolbox). That applying ethics includes all the four elements mentioned above (a, b, c, and d), is again not a matter of theoretical jugglery rather, it is getting involved in applying ethics in the society, in reality. If we are not involved in it, we can never know that ethics has tremendous applicative or practical value. That we apply ethical theories in reality, is matter of discovery, a discovery stemming out of actual participation in intersubjective corroboration. Applying ethics is thus not merely choosing one theory or the other to solve a problem but to bring people having ethical knowledge and ethical experience together to face moral impasse and to frame practical rules having moral value. Applying ethics may be thus included within a moral philosophy, which is moral because it does not let moral philosophy do mere mental gymnastics; it brings ethical knowledge into action, not in isolation but in cooperation. Let us try to do this in a democratic set-up to discover that normative ethical theories may be really applied by us. It is a matter of grave concern that even after almost sixty years of the progress of applied ethics, we do not understand that in the expression "applied ethics", "ethics" is not "ethical theories", it is something more. The main tone of applied ethics is applying ethical knowledge aided by intersubjective corroboration to resolve moral crisis. Again, "ethical knowledge" is not to be taken as "knowledge of ethical theories" it is rather the knowledge of the different valuable ways in which social beings face moral dilemmas and resolve them. Moral knowledge includes the knowledge of the valuable ways in which social beings judge intentional actions for their moral worth. Interestingly, the moral knowledge of the non-philosophers may reflect the features of what has been outlined in an ethical theory. This is a matter of ethical importance, which an ethicist may discover and let others know about it. If there are incongruities involved in an ethical theory or theories, an ethicist may persuade others to see it and have necessary changes in their moral views. When we participate in such a corrective process, one enriches one's ethical knowledge.

However, the analysts may not be satisfied because they may not believe that people have the "moral authority" to apply ethics and they may not believe that there may be 'value-laden problems'. The challenge of the analysts may be framed as follows—'philosophers have no moral authority'. In fact, nobody has that authority. Hence, it is pointless to speak of somebody having the authority to apply ethical theory. So why should philosophers in particular poke their nose in the business of other professionals and what if nobody applied ethics? J.L. Gorman puts this aptly in his paper, "Philosophical confidence" in J.D.G. Evans edited "*Moral Philosophy and Contemporary Problems*": "Analytic philosophers, if they are true to their training, never forget that first lesson of analytic philosophy—Philosophers have no moral authority... they never forget their second lesson of analytical philosophy either, nobody else has any moral authority".[11]

The problem is why should the analysts think that applying ethics is to conceive of somebody having an 'authority' to call into service the moral theories to solve practical problems having a moral dimension? Yes, it is true that neither philosophers nor non-philosophers are sole authorities of application of ethics. Yet, it is true that both may have enough ground for corroborating their views to apply ethical theories. Interestingly, applying ethics does not presuppose any authority as such it however demands intersubjective corroboration. The basis of the application of ethics by philosophers and non-philosophers is that ethical theories are not theoretical constructions to contemplate upon rather; they have great worth in solving moral impasse to take moral decision and to frame practical rules. However, the fact that a moral ideal is valuable enough to resolve moral dilemma is not the same thing as thinking that moral ideal is best suited for the resolution of all problems. That this is true is also a matter of experience and well-reasoned thinking. That moral ideal actually contributes to achieving the quality of human life is a matter of experience and well-reasoned thinking. Holistic knowledge of morality and living a moral life are both crucial in morality. Living a moral life is what is directly related to the application of ethics (in the sense in which I have been speaking). This truth has to be grasped by the analysts; otherwise analyzing moral language will take us nowhere. To ask the question, 'who has this authority?' is in a bad taste because no one has such an authority. Nevertheless, we try to find enough confidence in moral decision-making. This confidence comes from the range of moral knowledge and corroboration of moral views. This transcends the barriers of individual and specific professional knowledge. Applied ethics is thus a cooperative effort or effort of collective mind and corroboration among different professionals. It thus demands the possibility of collective morality and interdisciplinary corroboration of views regarding a practical problem in society that has a moral face. Ethicists are not vanguards of applied ethics, nor are the non-philosophers ultimate authorities. It is grossly immoral to think of ethicists having sole right to apply ethics is evident when we realize that an ethicist may be very wise in thinking about morality, an ethicist may contribute a lot with regard to resolve moral impasse but applying ethics demands to think outside myself concentrating on the collective venture and identifying collective decision with my own. It may well be that the collective decision may be like my own decision. It may be with little difference or with great change. One thing is for sure that it will bear a great value in a moral world. This also speaks of the fact that collective decisions may be changing, growing, regressing, progressing and so on. One who does not realize that there can be collective decisions (in which ethicists are active corroborators) fails to understand that collective may be "a party, or a nation, or a class, may have interest which are quite distinct from the interests either of a given individual or even of all the individuals who go to compose it at a given time."[12] It may be that in certain cases, an individual may be said to be morally charged, may be so morally correct in deciding what ought to be done, and yet, does conflict with the collective morality, but that person also has to corroborate his views with others so that the collective morality changes the older garb. Application of ethics is thus a constant social enterprise helping us to take moral decisions, which are worth following in this period at least and in the world, we live in. It may not be without individuals; however, it has to transcend individual and professional knowledge barriers. Most important is that in doing so, our basis is moral experience and moral interaction.

We must understand that ethics without applied ethics is phoenix ethics, merely formal, and contemplative. It does not come closer to our practical life and it does not help us—it is useless. Practical ethics is on the other hand an active enterprise, coming closer to life, to face real life situations. It does not make us moral but does help us to dispel moral hunches and to make us active participants of a moral world. It corrects us and reforms our moral views. It is thus highly useful. If we include this, ethics is useful ethics. Analysts should understand this. They should understand that without conceiving the homosapiens as social beings and without serious concern about their quality of life, morality is barren. We, therefore, need practical ethics to improve the moral life of the homosapiens. Hence, discarding it is dangerous because we are encouraging moral philosophy, which does no good to all of us rather, encourage a band of ethicists in satisfying their mental gymnastics

However, we must understand that applying ethics makes no sense if we do not look into the starting point of this venture. We need to apply ethics only when we face certain practical problems, which raise moral questions as well. We may call them value-laden problems. Let me give one example from a real life situation. Readers may recollect at this point that I had earlier mentioned about a 'stark truth', i.e. without moral experience, we cannot engage in any task of ethics. I have arranged discussion on "Should we harness rivers for power generation?" The obvious reason was that according to me this is not simply a practical problem faced by the electrical engineers rather it is a problem which attracts many of us because it raises moral question of the nature, "whether or not it is morally desirable to take such a practical decision in our society? Hence the word 'should' present in the above problem does not reflect whether or not it is practically valuable for us to get involved in such an action rather, whether or not such an action has a moral value. The question carried this distinct moral overtone because none of us (politicians, policy makers, engineers) can decide to do something, which affects other adversely. We may doubt that such an action may be detrimental to the quality of human life (and let us remember that the quality of human life is not disassociated from the sustenance of the ecological community of which we are members). We do really think that it is not ethically permissible to allow some people in the society to take decisions in favour of harnessing rivers for generating power. When I talked to many people in this regard, I was astonished to find that electrical engineers, social activists, politicians, economists, botanists and administrators, all agreed that a practical decision might have a moral face when we think carefully about this matter. All of them felt that a decision making practical rule should be ethically thought out. The panel was unanimous that power production by ruthlessly harnessing big rivers should not be allowed. Hence, such an act should be discarded as immoral for it is against the basic principle of sustainable ecological development. These people agreed that the basic principle, which is the guiding ideal in taking such practical decision with regard to these value-laden ecological problems, should be taken care of. This ideal is not devoid of the ideas of the 'creed of the human beings to develop' and 'the need of the poor'. We may further analyze to find that the guiding principle pronounced above reflects the basic features of a teleological ethical theory, which we call 'welfarism'. However, the panel did not only justify why such an act is immoral and undesirable, it helped in framing some decision making rules having moral face so that the moral problem can be efficiently resolved. The panelists were keen that the government agencies should know about it and common people join the chorus of protest.

Obviously, some problems, which we encounter in real life, are value-laden or are problems that raise moral questions. We may face moral impasse or moral crisis, which has to be resolved. To do so, applying ethics is what is crucial and that is made possible only if we corroborate our moral point of view to frame practical decision-making rules. If all this is done, professional decisions are ethically charged and are humane. A group, a party, a community and a nation can take recourse to this activity. Now that I am actively engaged in such an activity, I assure you, it works. Only thing is to have a democratic set-up, proper education and proper political will to make it a social creed.

Hence, I conclude that the proper task of ethics is to engage in normative and metaethical enquiry and to apply ethics to resolve value-laden problems. Practical ethics is thus within ethics and is useful for us only if we choose that right methodology. In fact, much confusion in applying ethics is due to the lack of the knowledge of proper methodology. What I prefer is, "inter-subjective corroboration", to which we shall come later on. Let us conclude that ethics consists of applied ethics. Moreover to our 'nagging question' we now have an answer that ethics does have a practical or pragmatic face and the decision making rules are not thumb rules of ethical action or mere do-don't type guidelines. These decision-making rules make sense in the context of professional ethics in particular. But to know more about it, one has to know what is "professional ethics", how it is related to "application of ethics" and what are the importance of the decision making rules.

NOTES

1. Readers may refer to P.H. Nowell-Smith's work, *Ethics* which explains the different functions of ethical language.

2. This is the position of Rudolf Carnap in *The Unity of Science* (Trans.) Max, Black, Kegan Paul, Trench, Turbner Co. Ltd., London, 1934, p. 24.
3. Ayer, A.J., *Language, Truth and Logic*, O.U.P., N.Y., 1935, p. 150.
4. *Ibid.*, p. 150.
5. *Ibid.*, p. 158.
6. Stevenson, C.L., *Ethics and Language*, Yale Univ. Press, New Haven, 1944, p. VII.
7. Schlick, M., *Problems of Ethics*, (Trans.) D. Rynia, Henry-Holt, N.Y., 1939, p. 78.
8. *Ibid.*, p. 17.
9. Readers may refer to the view of John Dewey in this regard in this *Human Nature and Conduct*, Henry-Holt & Co., N.Y., 1922, p. 326.
10. Kimpel, Ben, *Principles of Moral Philosophy*, Philosophical Library, N.Y., 1974, p. 103.
11. Evans, J.D.G. (ed), *Moral Philosophy and Contemporary Problems*, Cambridge University Press, 1982, p. 71.
12. Graham, Keith in Evans J.D.G. (ed), *Moral Philosophy and Contemporary Problems, ibid.*, p. 15.

2

Practical Ethics and Professional Ethics

Readers at this stage might wonder. You have told us what is Applied Ethics or Practical Ethics leaving an important discussion about the methodology of ethical application (which you nevertheless said is most crucial); you have also mentioned that applied ethics, normative ethics and metaethics all form a coherent whole called 'ethics'. We assume that these are the three important branches of ethics, a field not to be confused with moral science. However, what are the branches of applied or practical ethics? Alternatively, do we imagine that it has no branch?

First, we must understand that answering our readers' fresh set of questions is to tell clearly about the tasks of applied ethics because a clear idea about these tasks will give us a clear idea about the important branches of applied ethics. Let us take an example. A professional doctor, a teacher, or a lawyer faces several value-laden practical problems in their day-to-day social encounter. There is no way but to face these problems with sincerity and care or else they have to tarnish their nature as a social being and most likely, their essential professional nature will be at stake. How can a nephrologist go on avoiding the problem that among several recipients of kidneys, should he take on priority basis the affluent class who can pay high price for it? If neglect is the answer, we know what gradually dawn on our poor doctor. He is most likely tend to neglect the ethical question to settle for what his conscience tells him best, and he may tend to believe that his call of conscience is utterly moral and his decision is moral as well. Does he have any regard for the medical fraternity, the patients and the number of families? No perhaps. In addition, this neglect for such ethical impasse converts him to a heartless, mindless professional, completely disliked by many of us in the society, including fellow doctors for the simple reason that he does not care to think that many people around him do care for such ethical questions seriously, before a crucial decision is taken. However if we care for such moral problems, it contributes to the well-being of the professional life. Is it just for this reason that the doctor need not go for unnecessary moral scrutiny? Not at all because a factual problem need not be morally neutral. Moral problems do have factual anchor, they do not drop from the blue. Hence, to think that a factual problem raises no special ethical problem to a doctor is to imagine that some people have an ugly habit to make some problems morally value-laden by sheer whims. Problems are not made value-laden by us; they are realized like that once we start considering the "desirability" aspect of these problems. To compare, we may have another problem for the doctors. The problem is, whether or not a doctor should ask kidney recipient to pay a social visit to the donor to pay his heartfelt gratitude. This problem is factual, or it is practical but does not raise the same level of "desirability" question, as does the former one. Thus, our professional doctor should take care of some value laden problems, which they face in their professional life because they raise serious questions of "moral desirability".

What happens when the professionals, like our caring doctor faces such value-laden problems? Clearly, they strive for a moral resolution for practical decision making which are morally charged. However, moral resolution is not a mechanical affair for there are no thumb-rules for resolution. We have to go for, what I said, intersubjective corroboration because the problem should not be treated by a professional in utter isolation (otherwise the same conscience-type confusion creeps in). Thus, moral resolution involves other parties and meaningful moral dialogue. Here, in this process, what our professionals and other parties do is simple application of their ethical knowledge (not necessarily ethical theories). We may, therefore, conclude that our professionals do have several ethical considerations and this takes us to the application of ethics. What is clear is that professional ethical consideration is one task under ethics, which is closely related to applied ethics. To be precise, applied ethics takes on the task of ethical application in professional life. Hence, one branch of applied ethics is professional ethics, *appears to be true*. We will come to see that business ethics is believed to be another branch, sports ethics the other one, environmental ethics a very stimulating one, and then we have a plenty of them; medical ethics, legal ethics and so on. Each having independent existence for their unique ethical consideration but most (not all) should be included within practical ethics in so far as all fields mentioned above do nothing but apply ethics in the sense in which I have advocated applied ethics. I would like to stress again that if applied ethics is mechanical or engineering type, how ethics is applied in the form of theoretical manipulation is not known to me. It is absurd. I shall come to it in the next chapter.

There will be no difficulty in maintaining that professional ethics is within ethics but to call it a branch of applied ethics, as is the case of medical ethics, needs some examination. (Let us remember that once we start this analysis. It is essentially meta-ethical, and therefore, the tasks of ethics are not unrelated). First, we have to know about "profession" which is explained well in many books, but for simplicity one can go through Timo Airaksinen's essay in *Encyclopedia of Applied Ethics Vol. III.* The talk about "profession" is relatively new. In older societies and in primitive ones people did not care much about a "professional man" because those societies were permeated with typical "primary group" relationship, which means man-to-man contact, an intimacy, which is informal and close to our heart. However, in the older societies there were some professionals. A person treating the sick and the other teaching his pupils and so on. Nevertheless, we never thought so seriously about giving these people a name to construct a profession related talk. Only in the modern times, where our life is complex and we are constantly in contact with several "secondary groups",[1] we have felt the need of talking about "profession", "professions" and "professional man". The secondary groups are distance-maintaining groups, where a meeting between people is need oriented or service oriented. A meeting lasting not so long. May be for once in a life time and quite likely, the dictates of give-and-take in terms of services and payment are supreme. In such complex interpersonal social relationship, we do feel to construct "professional talk".

What is unique in these peculiar modern societies is the phenomenal growth of occupations, labour, and job division along with specialization. The importance of "tasks as per specialization" has grown tremendously and with it has lived a philosophy— "to each one according to his specialization and each one free to earn as much as he can". The complex society with these people having quietly nurturing benefits in their heads was called professionals. However, that does not mean that each one got what he or she wanted to get. Nevertheless, completely social life was seen in fragments. The philosophy of life being "people come and go but I shall extract whatever benefits suit me". The commercialization and the regard for human welfare were thus inversely related in their minds. Nevertheless, that does not mean that one should stop talking about human welfare, social welfare and ethical concerns in such a commercialized professional life. One, who cared such things, constructed another dimension to the "professional talk", viz., the "ethics-talk in professions". Many people thus started thinking (without seriously disregarding personal benefits and the value of commerce) about the ethical value of the professional life and about the number of ethical problems ensuing within a professional life.

However, the professionals have their own problems before plunging into social, humane, moral etc. considerations. They have their own rules and methods of working, which are according to their basic needs and not that of the society because it is very difficult for a professional at the outset to frame benevolent rules and methods of working. Next, the professionals are self-governed people, who prefer least social or institutional interference in their work because that would fail to promote their immediate commercial interest. However, people talking about the ethics of professionalism, would argue that a professional man is first a social man, whatever may be the present complex structure of the contemporary society. These people must understand that all professionalism vanish when the market eludes them with the eluding buyers or the clients. So why should the professionals not care for the society before taking commercial or benefit-making decisions? Why should they not care for what is desirable and what is undesirable before constructing their rules and methods of working? Therefore, a profession related talk involves ethics-talk as well. There may be more reasons in favour of this in a civilized society. With the growth of intricate professions demanding high skill and knowledge, common person in the society are completely helpless when they are in need of these specialists. In addition, if whole working is left to the professionals, not standing the moral concerns, and if there is not least public check and interference, the public will be fooled and harmed to limits not known to us. Therefore, we do have to care for social and ethical questions in professional conduct. With this, we come to know that when we talk about profession, professions and professional man we are in fact considering two things at a time. We are considering some such problems which make great sense in the field sociology, and we are considering some such problems which make great sense in the field of ethics. However, before we come to "professional ethics", we have to analyze for the clear meaning of "profession", "professionalism" etc. that are very important sociologically speaking and ethically speaking. I am indebted to the analysis of time Airaksinen in this regard.

If we take another oblique turn, we first consider what a "profession" is not. We have a tendency to confuse "profession" with "business" and think that a profession amounts to being involved in some business. We have seen that in olden times or even in modern days, someone having a profession is believed to be aiming at personal financial benefits and nothing else. So the ideal of business is like profession, purely financial profiteering, and for that reason both have the same connotation. Moreover, business and profession are both commercial activities fundamentally. There is hardly any need to draw an imaginary line of distinction between the two. Nevertheless, there are basic problems in such thinking. First, business is one full time engagement and not the only one, for we do speak of many professional engagements which, unlike commercial business activities, do something more, i.e., they not merely aim at personal financial profiteering. They have different ideals. Many such professions have "service ideal" as primary rather than putting financial ideal at the top. Therefore, it will be too narrow to call "profession", a "business" because it has financial ideal only. Further, not all professional activities are purely commercial. In fact, many professional activities are something more than commercial as far as such activities are concerned more about social benefit, public welfare, and regard for desirability questions and so on. It is not true to say that, business activities are purely commercial as far as they completely disregard social welfare and desirability questions. However, the difference lies in giving relative importance to service ideal, human welfare and moral concern in professions and to commercial manipulation, financial gains, and personal well-being in business. This is to say that some degree of ethical concern may be involved in business or commercial activities as well, and it is for this reason that apart from professional ethics, we do speak of business ethics. Moreover, here is the meeting ground—both may involve ethics-talk and thus within practical ethics and broadly within ethics. The meeting grounds are many. It will be too wide to call "professions" as something having "service ideal" and "ethical concerns". Professions do involve a degree of personal concern, "financial benefits" apart from what we have already discussed. Hence, we must beware of either the too narrow or the too wide explanations of the notion of "profession". The former will lead us to a confusion that it is nothing but business, whereas the latter will lead us to the idea that it has nothing to do with profits and benefits. There is indeed a difference in the mode of commercial activities in business and professions. Most important is that the mode of earnings and profiteering are different. Generally, the professional man is dependent on earnings, salaries, or incentives which have a limit fixed normally by different institutions or which gets limited by the different self-imposed practical restrictions or by the different social, economic and political forces. However the "service as rendered is found where the professional man bases his charges upon the time and energy and skill which he finds it necessary to give".[2] However, in case of business, the upper limit of earning, profits etc. is the sky, for the freedom is self-imposed mainly, and governed by the basic philosophy of "as much as you can". Therefore, there is a stiff resistance to extrinsic or other intellectual restrictions to earning. One cannot rule out the possibility that in this full-freedom syndrome in business, ethical concern is bogus. The point is that we should better have such concern. In view of all these points we may now say that although a "profession" is not merely a "business", it is essentially "service ideal" oriented engagement of social-persons having restricted benefit-making intentions. We can also mention that although it makes some sense to speak of "business ethics" (many think that there is no ethics in business), and it is believed that the profiteering-syndrome is at its worst form at times (some want to lower it nevertheless). Therefore, there is no profession called "business", and this may be a tragic note to those enthusiasts who would like to utter them synonymously or even treat business ethics as a branch of professional ethics. With this, it is clear that business ethics cannot be a branch of professional ethics. Again, one would imagine that "engineering" is a good case of "profession". Is "engineering" a profession? Alternatively, can we make people understand what a "profession" is by citing the instance of "engineering"? Let me justify that the instance is not so good for understanding what a "profession" is because "engineering" in reality is "profession wrongly so called" or to be precise, "pseudo-profession". The reasons in favour of justifying engineering as a pseudo-profession may be mainly drawn from whatever has been already said in the context of "business". However, in the case of "engineering", the reasons should be a little different that the vagueness in our minds about not considering engineering a profession may be far too stiff. However, we must first speak about "service ideal" as the primary connotation to identify "profession". Engineering is a pseudo-profession insofar as it has no "service ideal" as such. One may wonder because engineers are believed to have a "service ideal". Can we identify such commonly agreeable ideal as we can do easily in case of medical profession? The medical man has an important service ideal, namely, "promotion of public health". Teachers have a professional service ideal, namely, "public education". What ideal is before engineers? Interesting fact is that a primary teacher, a higher secondary teacher or a post-graduate teacher all mingles together in an occupational milieu to educate not merely himself or his close ones only but the public. The ideal is set primarily not for earning or profit making only but for public welfare as well. Similarly, cardiologists, radiologists, anesthetists or whatever, they are having service ideal, viz. "promotion of public health". Nevertheless, what is the general service ideal, that too for the general welfare primarily (and profiteering secondarily), in case of the engineers? Can we imagine a service ideal common to an electrical engineer, a civil engineer, a software engineer and so on? Perhaps it is difficult to set such an ideal. Let us imagine that the ideal is, "construction" or "designing" or "design and construction". Let us argue that they are for the public, no doubt for their welfare. In addition, let us allow that all this is done under income-restrictions and free profiteering is not allowed. Some engineers do design, frame a plan, construct a blueprint and so on but not all of them do such things. An architect may be primarily doing such things, may be an environmental engineer does such things but a software engineer may be doing completely different set of things. Hence, within the *occupation* called "engineering", we imagine several cases of sub-occupations each having important ideals but not one. Further, engineers' work may be largely for the public and not for mere profiteering but within that occupation we do have large section of engineers vying for "profits only" as the chief ideal for these people are doing a business and not having a profession. Hence, an engineering occupation may be public oriented, as if giving a plan for a dam but there may be one planner of dam who had this occupation of pure business, and not under any internal or intellectual as well as external restrictions mentioned by me. Therefore, the case of engineering occupation is very complex. Still more, all engineers do not construct because that occupation may be of daily wage earners as well. Now if we take "to construct" as not merely "to build" rather, to "make a design", such "constructions" may not be undertaken by all engineers. Even if someone takes it up seriously, it may well be that it is his or her business and not a public oriented or welfare directed work. Therefore, in that case it will be very difficult to call "engineering" a "profession". Airaksinen Timo brings out this unique distinction between the "classic professions" (service-ideal oriented) and "engineering occupation" by saying that, "engineers relationship to a service ideal and its values are problematic, or at least they must be understood differently from the classic professions. The key issue here is the service ideal, what kind of value-based service is provided by the engineers."[3]

It would be a little shocking for our serious engineers having restricted income (particularly in public institutions), to digest the truth that what they have is at best an "occupation" but not a profession. They may argue that for them safety, public welfare are the service ideals. However, they forget that these ideals are at best constraints rather than goals in engineering. In fact, such engineers should be convinced that they are at least serving an employer by producing good designs and so on that allows the employers to achieve different goals. Quite often, the "goodness" of their designs is judged by intrinsic standards of engineering and not by an ideal as thinks the so-called public engineers. Nevertheless, a serious and honest engineer (public or private) should keep human or social welfare in mind apart from their intrinsic demands and secondary constraints. However, this is no moral obligation on them, not an imperative in any sense. In addition, this makes it so different from the "classic service-ideal" oriented professions "like teaching". The relation between an engineer who produces (a design for instance), an employer who obtains (or even purchase), and a client who buys or draws an indirect benefit (like living in a well-designed house) is extremely different from a teacher, his employer and his clients (pupils). Nevertheless, as was the case of business, there is nothing wrong or absurd in talking about what should be done and what should not be done in an engineering occupation. Clearly, an engineering occupation may associate ethical consideration. However, for this we have to imagine a separate branch of applied ethics viz., "engineering ethics" (like business ethics) but these do not form a part of "professional ethics", for these are not "professions".

Nevertheless, can we speak of "a nursing profession"? On the other hand, can we cite an example of "nursing" in order to understand what "profession" is? Let us assume that nursing is a profession. Apart from other things essential for calling something a "profession", the most important factor is that it should have a definite "service ideal". What is the definite "service ideal" of nursing? The question appears to be a little amateurish to many because even common sense reflection would reveal that "promotion of public health" is the clear "service ideal" of nursing. In fact, the question is not at all amateurish and a reply so simple could be more like an amateur analyst. Because we have just discussed that "promotion of public health" or promotion of the biological well-being of the public in general is the "service ideal" of the medical profession, and it is that the ideal could be achieved by assimilating different *sub-professions* under the medical profession (which is the classic profession having the classic ideal).

We should have no doubt that in order to promote people's biological welfare we need doctors but we need nurses (male and female) to do a specific or specialized job, viz., taking care of the pre- and post-operative, patients as well as critically ill to moderately ill people who are under general medicine. Nurses may be further assisted by chemists, dressers, midwives, ward attendants and so on, they may all come under the "care-taking unit" if we wish to coin this term. However, the doctors, diagnosing, prescribing and operating along with "care-taking" people do not end up the whole profession called, the "medical profession". Many of us nurture this poor idea that medical researchers, pathologists, radiologists, those dealing with medical engineering, and the entire gamut of "malady detecting and cure finding" units are under the medical profession. I have some reservations to call "medical representatives", medical man because their occupation is more to assist the business ideal of their employers (medicine magnets). We may have another hesitation in calling "medicine educators" or "medical teachers" under the medical profession because here the superimposing ideal is that of the teacher, i.e. "imparting knowledge" (specialized nevertheless). Therefore, we may speak about them having a teaching profession. Similar is the case of "drug-educators" in drug companies because they serve the business ideal of their employers indirectly. We may face such hesitation in putting physiologists within the medical profession although they are concerned with specific systematic knowledge contributing to people's biological well-being. However, more than that, physiologists may be contributing to the biological well-being of other animals as well. More importantly, they are directly related to profession of knowledge acquiring and knowledge imparting about life forms. Therefore, they have a different occupation, not a profession as we may think. However, that does not prevent them from being researchers and teachers, and if they take a physiology-teaching task, they are having a "teaching profession". However, one who is a researcher, as may be the case with a medical-researcher; he or she does not have this profession, rather a sub-profession. A researcher, who happens to be a teacher, is having a "teaching profession". A researcher, who happens to be a doctor, is having "medical profession". Therefore, "research" is their sub-profession. Similarly, is the case with nursing, as it contributes to the medical professions' greater ideal, and mainly benevolent and only partially under the influence of income and earning, they have a sub-profession. However, it is never a pseudo-profession as is with the engineering. There may be an interesting debate regarding someone pursuing nothing but full-time research, and if this were the case, can we call him or her having a "research profession"? I have an idea that any occupation demanding research is a sub-profession contributing to a field's general ideal or it is an independent occupation contributing to a field's different ideal but 'what this ideal is' is difficult to ascertain, as it is difficult to imagine research without other engagements.

We may now come to a closure mentioning the fact that "profession" is not business, and we must be careful about confusing "profession" with "sub-profession" and "pseudo-profession". We have another conception, i.e., most importantly, profession is an engagement having a "service ideal" in which several intrinsic restrictions are put to check and balance egoistic benefits. However, there are other important elements in clarifying the notion of "profession". I think we are aware of these elements. One is that profession is a specialized or skilled engagement, and therefore, restricted to a limited group of people, who can perform a task extremely efficiently than others in their lifetime. They seldom deviate from such skills.[4] These elements have been put by Timo Airaksinen as follows; "a profession is a number of exclusive group of individuals who possess a value-based service ideal, and have abstract knowledge of their own field. Professionalism is the relevant ideology with its behavioural and policy-oriented counterparts."[5]

If we go on analyzing the meaning of "profession" and "professionalism", we come to know that a profession demands an accurate knowledge of the basic facts, which are the corner stone of professional activities. The knowledge need not be merely dormant or static; it needs to be applied or practical. Nevertheless, an amateur may be as knowledgeable as a professional of a particular field but we have to make a clear distinction between the two by closely scrutinizing those members engaged in a specialized activity who are more or less permanent members of that group activity. An amateur may not be so permanent in terms of dedication and application, and quite often may replace the service ideal with personal dignity and rewards without however accepting the basic responsibility naturally incumbent on the professional. Moreover, an amateur may not only commit more errors in judgments, decision, action etc., they may fail to analyze the points to decide and may not readily accept a defeat or a more foolproof method of revival. All this is due to the lack of the service ideal. No doubt, a profession is a way to earn a living, and to earn sufficient comfort and peace of mind, which is due to all citizens in a free civil life. Nevertheless, what is foremost to them is their ideal of public service and not profiteering for personal physical upliftment. For this several restriction, external and internal are allowed by a professional to pursue the path of noble service. So professionalism becomes an ideology for a profession, which means, he is prepared to go for a skilled behavioural pattern in society to contribute to the human well-being but in due course, he respects what is due to him. "Professionalism" is often derogated to mean doing what is best to a person and not to the work as such. However, we cannot know that "professionalism" takes care for the quality of the work first because profiteering is at the backseat. He or she wants to display his or her skill to the highest level for a quality of work fitted to the quality of human life. We can see that "profession" and "professionalism" cares for the ethical questions primarily as an ethical desirable ideal along with ethically desirable decision-making. Therefore, it is but natural to speak of "professional ethics". We shall come to it later on. Let us go on with "professionalism" a little farther. The derogatory use of this term hints at a self-caring person as I have mentioned. "These days teachers have become too professional", we often come across such remarks. One of my friends cracked a joke. A teacher while giving a private tuition course replaced "white washing" with "lime-giving", when asked about it, the teacher replied "with the amount paid, white-washing is lime-giving". According to Plato, every professional is a possessor of 'opposite capacities'. A doctor treats as well as kills. What a teacher can do, we know. However, let me make clear that these are all "professionalism" wrongly understood. These are at best "amateurism" or even a gross caricature of professionalism. Because "professionalism" implies putting the self to the second place and strive best to provide unbiased and dedicated attention to public well-being. Let us know that when a doctor kills for the sake of money, he is no professional doctor, a "killer" nevertheless. What service ideals do professions have or what are the professional ideologies of professional people? Are nevertheless, interesting inquiries.

Apart from the basic ideal, we may thus speak of dedicated service for clients "welfare" within acceptable limits as one important ideal. This reminds us of the fact that professionalism involves moral and intellectual virtues. Among intellectual virtues, we may speak of skilled, effective reasoning, communicating, choosing among alternatives and applying abstract knowledge to practical problems. Among moral virtues we may conceive, dedicated service for the cause of people (who are clients), feeling of compassion and an empathetic involvement with the client's endeavour notwithstanding concern for justice whatever may be the dangers, temptations and challenges. Because respect for promises made is most essential. The other moral ideals may be, respect for autonomy, privacy, truthfulness, humility and objectivity.[6] Given these moral worth, one assumes how important it will be to talk of ethical concerns in professions. Among other ideals of professionalism, we may speak of making a legitimate balance in the face of tension between internal goods and external goods because a professional is concerned with both kinds of goods, and there is evident danger in overplaying with any one of them. The "internal goods" of a profession may be unique to it. For instance, the internal good of a teaching profession may be finding out a proper model or methodology of teaching. Let us imagine that the methodology so discovered is to hold classroom debates among students and teachers regarding a problem, so that in the near future the subject teachers may be benefited by the contributions made to the field by the teacher. Nevertheless, teacher takes interest in some "external goods" as well. For instance, he may take interest in his pupils getting a sound knowledge of the problem in consideration and secure good marks as well. If we take pupils to be clients, then the "external goods" is the clients' good whereas the "internal good" is good for the teacher and the subject he teaches. A professional has to think about both goods and if he overplays with one, the other is neglected which results in "non-professionalism" in the part of the teacher. So serving one's ownself, one's own subject, and one's own service group people and to serve clients judiciously is another ideal in professionalism. Therefore, an excellent professional is the one who in his lifetime has successfully balanced the internal and the external goods, otherwise either a substandard client service or a substandard discipline or group service is in the offing. It is here again that ethical concern in profession and professionalism is clear because we are forced to think that caring about moral responsibilities and duties towards oneself and towards others in a judicious manner may be crucial in professionalism.

However, the conflict between personal ideals and professional ideals demand another thing from the professional. It is to maintain perfect integrity as a professional or to remain completely unbiased. If we go by the basic service ideal of professions we find that as far as he is a professional, he should give prime importance to the role-responsibility bestowed on him not overlooking his personal ideals. But personal ideals like "being a teacher who never gives private tuitions to this own pupils" may be justified to a great extent whereas another ideal like "never teaching those who are not admitted to his own institution" may be unjustified and dogmatic. A professional teacher or whatever should display perfect integrity in compromising with such conflicts. One has to make a judicious accommodation to legitimate demands of other justified ideals and responsibilities in professional life, otherwise dogmatism will follow. Here again one can see that in the face of such conflict, several ethical questions become prominent. Hence, any disregard to ethical concern in professionalism is harmful. Another ideal related problem arises for the professionals when they are faced with *supererogatory tasks*. Here again the clash is between the personal and the professional life. The problem is more acute in so far as it has far more deep ethical impact because we ask what is desirable in exceeding the 'role responsibilities' bestowed on a professional? Is it not immoral to have satisfied one's predilections by exceeding the responsibilities given to a professional within his subject or field? Therefore, we have the sense that some minimum responsibilities are bestowed on professionals. Given their service ideal, some responsibilities are optional and well within the basic ideal and some are self-decided to cross the limits or to fix new limits to the erstwhile fixed ideals. Nevertheless, to fix such new ideals may be more self-fulfilling or to some people self-satisfying. What is great in doing all that? Professional services being highly specialized and to great extent monopoly services, clients in the society have every moral right to raise the questions of honesty, justice, equal treatment and so on. Given this high demand scenario, a professional need not turn the pages of his codebook and fixed set of rules laid down by his group to satisfy public demands. Wisdom lies in contextual decision-making and on several institutional factors like whether or not alternatives are available in giving the best to the public even at the cost of transgressing the orthodox rules and tasks. Yes, a good professional should open out in fully favouring the case of his client, where "good" is the moral good, i.e. the well-being that is due to his client and that which is desirable. For this, he should recognize the importance of few supererogatory conducts in selecting a core group of benefactors. However, he may not be able to expand the horizon forever and go on doing the supererogatory tasks too far because that robs off some of his zeal in performing his basic tasks, and this is not ethical. There is no doubt that a government college teacher in India should coolly take on the responsibility to teach a core group of his regular pupils during his free time who are not finding things very easy or are facing stiff problems in understanding along with better off students in the classroom. Nevertheless, this cannot go on forever. A time may come when you do a little too much to hamper your personal as well as professional ideals. So a balance in needed. A sense of 'where to stop' is essential. In fact, as we find in this example, the question is whether supererogatory responsibilities are desirable or morally optional. The tension can be settled easily if we keep in mind the fact that both personal and professional ideals are important for a professional, and as such, a professional should respect his personal responsibilities largely. Then a serious sensitive professional (our college teacher) finds it incumbent on him to call his poor students when he has some free time to repeat his course so that they are able to catch up others. Although for one poor student who would never catch up, you cannot regularly do such things. There is no point to agree with J.O. Urmson that supererogatory performers are either saints or heroes and to argue that they have crossed their moral bindings as professionals. So professional supererogatory actions are not heroic rather they are needed at times. The matter is one of balance and judgment. One thing is clear, even this discussion reminds us of the fact that professional ideals may unfold a number of important ethical trifles for us.

The example of our college teacher gives us another idea about what is the nature of professional ideal. If a professional imagines that, his clients demand a high degree of self-sacrifice in realizing the service ideal then he is mistaken. Choosing a profession, accepting the duties and responsibilities naturally incumbent on the professional does not mean that from day one, the professional should inculcate a habit of self-sacrifice, i.e., sacrificing his professional goals for the more benevolent acts. The most benevolent you become, the better professional you are, is the message perhaps. However, this benevolence is living in a fool's paradise because pure benevolence or even pure self-interest can never lead us to self-realization. The best champions of self-realization would not argue that a professional should grab every opportunity to do benevolent work at the cost of the growth of his personal skill and professional ability. One has to know that as a professional he or she has to maintain and flourish some of his or her basic skills and abilities and not to indulge in egalitarian overdoing. By doing such things, even professional service ideals become a little blurred. There is no doubt that when we pick a professional career we should be well aware of our duties, rights and responsibilities towards our clients and we should have personal goals set in our professional life as well. One such goal may be self-fulfilment through realization of the service ideal. However, this is not the same as self-fulfilment through self-sacrifice. We should know that self-fulfilment could be obtained through maintaining a judicious balance in one's professional life between his internal and external ideals. This can be attained in a number of ways. A list not so comprehensive may be prepared for this, lest we remember that self-fulfilment should never be confused with self-satisfaction because our satisfaction levels are not known to us and the basic service ideal may easily be in conflict with personal predilections, and no self-realization is possible. When a professional realizes his true self, he discovers that he is a sane head who can do what is primarily expected from him, i.e., doing the best for his clients through putting internal and external self-imposed restrictions, which are so needed, and by realizing the personal cherished goals of excellence and honing skills and talent. It is here again we find scope for moral discussion pertaining to professional ideal. Therefore, what is interesting to notice is that the very nature of profession and professionalism is such that it allows a number of ethical discussions. We shall now take on this interesting discussion, i.e., the discussion of "professional ethics". This is rather important for us insofar as our main objective has been professional ethics as a branch to practical ethics.

Now that the ground is prepared, we should know what "professional ethics" is and then discuss why it is within practical ethics. To understand what is "professional ethics", we must first know that it is an ethical discussion pertaining to professions and professionalism. It may mean something more. We can speak of codified morals for professionals under professional ethics. However to have more clear idea about it, we must first of all know that it is a sheer misconception to think that "ethics" in "professional ethics" is the same as "morality". In professional ethics, we do not merely talk about a few morals, like what a professional should do or should not do in codified forms to enable them in their practical life to take efficient decisions. We do not disagree that this may be a part of knowing about what is professional ethics but this is not all. A discussion about morals and morality may include many things of social and legal concern, therefore, it is not exclusively about profession and professionalism. We may say that professional ethics pays attention to several questions relating to ideals, goals, norms, rights, duties, responsibilities and goodness within the broad ethical realm. Any discussion in the field of professions, which raises the problems of desirability, ought, justice and moral right, may be said to fall within the field of professional ethics. Naturally, professional ethics is meaningful in the context of a core group and does not cover discussions which overlap or superimpose each other. Any discussion about business ethics, nursing ethics and engineering ethics need not be considered within the discussion of professional ethics. It is clear therefore that for a meaningful ethical discussion regarding professions and professionalism, one should have a clear idea about the core group professionals and avoid any confusion. We must also know that apart from considering these basic theoretical aspects, professions should have a more practical orientation in codifying what is ethically expected of them or what should be their guiding ethical force reflecting the moral considerations of the core group towards several value-laden problems. However, such codifications are not the result of theoretical jugglery by a set of professional rather is obtained after a gruesome application of their ethical experience and ethical knowledge. When we delve into these practical considerations of ethics, we have another story—the story of applying ethics in different professions. Then we come to know that professional ethics involves application of ethical knowledge as well. We may now revise our earlier assertion about professional ethics by stating that "professional ethics" may involve at least a two-tier discussion. One is purely theoretical ethical discussion pertaining to professions and professionalism. The others the applicative part, where professionals apply their moral knowledge to resolve several value-laden practical problems with which they are concerned and may end up in framing professional ethical codes for decision-making and role-guiding. Therefore, we may now modify our earlier assertion by stating further that professional ethics is not merely within applied ethics, it is within the wider field of theoretical ethics. This needs more clarification. We have just seen that when we discuss about professions, service ideals and professionalism, we speak a lot about the ethical ends, means, the desirable goals, virtues, and about duties, responsibilities and other things, which come within normative ethical discussion. One who has no idea about the basics of normative ethics would hardly follow the professional ideals, duties and so on. However, there is something more. We may ask some basic questions like, why should we speak of such and such professional ideal and not other ideals? Why should we speak of such and such responsibilities? We may also ask, "what is the meaning of 'profession'?", "What is professionalism?", and "What is professional ethics?" First set of questions are the problems of justification in professional ethics, whereas the other set of questions are about classification of basic notions. Both taken together are metaethical in nature. Readers may be aware of the fact that what I have been doing in this chapter is essentially metaethical insofar as I have been considering clarification of basic notions so that we may cope up with the vocabulary of professional ethics. Indeed, we have not taken the other task of justification. We shall take it up shortly but not in the way of justifying such and such ideals or such and such responsibilities but more basic than that, namely, why is it sensible to speak or discuss about "professional ethics"? Why is it within applied ethics and ethics proper? As I have said in the earlier chapter if we avoid such questions, skeptics are the winners. It will take no time for them to declare that professional ethics is meaningless and hopeless.

So apart from normative ethical considerations, we do have metaethical considerations in professional ethics, which is clear to us now. Then we may claim that one part of our justification is clear as well, i.e., professional ethical discussion involves both meta-ethics and normative ethics or theoretical ethics in general, and we should not hesitate in saying that it is well within ethics. Shortly I shall take up the problem of justification in another way. For the applied part of professional ethics, we have to wait for the next chapter.

Nevertheless, before we come to justification, a few words about "professional ethics". Based on our earlier discussion we may say that professional ethics is such a field within ethics, which aims at governing the work of professionals in addition to set moral ideals for professionals. It is not true to say that mere legal binding and rules guide professional life, because a professional life depends on greater ethical considerations. It is perhaps due to this that there is an urgent need to have codified ethical decision-making rules emerging out of practical ethical endeavour of professionals. There are new vistas in a philosophical understanding of morality involved in professional life. We may have a serious philosophical analysis of professional values and obligations, powers of professions, the nature and validity of professional authority, and the moral questions related to the paternalistic attitude that professional is higher placed than clients in decision-making. We may have a philosophical analysis of the morality involved in clients' right, rights of the professionals and the case of privacy. Another important feature of professional ethics is the critical analysis of the nature of the role of the public in professional life and professionalism and the public scrutiny of professional works. Professional ethics as a general field may subsume many sub disciplines as ethics of work and quality-of-work-life. In these cases, professional ethics may concentrate on the philosophical analysis of moral questions regarding a paid occupation and about the value of a qualitatively good life of such occupants. We may discuss about the rights and duties of the paid occupations. Nevertheless, many ethicists believe that to discuss about ethics of work needs more care and elaboration. The reason is that work and profession may be treated completely differently.

From this, we have an idea that practical ethics may be treated in different ways by ethicists. Some of us may prefer to analyze it within applied ethics only, and there are people who go to the extreme claim that all we have is applied ethics and no professional ethics because professional ethics is nothing but application of ethical norms in professions and resolving value-laden problems in their practical life. There is no doubt that application of the ethical norms is very important but I have argued that it is, not all. Therefore, we may have different treatments within theoretical ethics as well. The theoretical approach may not be too interesting for the professionals for it may turn out to be highly demanding in terms of academic knowledge of normative ethics and metaethics, and in terms of picking up the excellence of a philosophical criticism. It may not be liked for it may be negative insofar as many professional decisions, acts, rights, duties, obligations and aspects of professionalism may be criticized thoroughly. However, that does not prevent us from a philosophical effort. We shall come to know later on that even practical interest in professions may not be completely devoid of a theoretical ethical adventure. Nevertheless, we shall suspend this discussion now. What I want to stress here is that professional ethics is an ethical discussion meaning an involvement of the whole gamut of ethics, theoretical and practical. Therefore, we conclude that it is within ethics. However, this conclusion may be fortified as we proceed to consider the methodology of applied ethics in the next chapter.

However, the fact that professional ethics is within ethics proper may be justified in another way. We know that professionals in modern civilized societies, have both internal and external goals set for themselves to strive because that does not merely fulfil their stereotype professional demands, they realize the true professional-self which is key to their survival, commitment and constant growth in ability and excellence. Therefore, the professionals should live for the realization of a good life through qualitative work. We may say that the quality of professional life is perceived through quality-of-work-life. Here, "good" means morally good, morally worthwhile, or morally desirable. Hence, "morally good life" and "quality-of-work-life" are the two most important professional virtues. Such a discussion of virtues stem out of ethics, particularly in "virtue ethics". An analysis of these basic professional virtues is thus one important task under theoretical ethics or moral philosophy. This is a different type of analysis of professional ethics because it leaves out the more traditional analysis of professional duties, rights, obligations and so on to take more care of professional virtues and professional moral character. We may call this a more modern approach in ethics to know more about the basic moral virtues underlying professions and professionalism. Given this modernity, many ethicists today do not prefer too much to delve into the conditions of professional duties, rights etc. which are thought to be morally oriented. People even disregard the overdoing with universalized principles and prescriptive deductions in an artificial manner in the professional life. We shall come to its defects in the next chapter. However, this modern approach is not bereft of the practical ethical orientation of professional ethics. It is rather the other way round. Giving more importance to the analysis of virtues and character of professionals, is basically intended to let the professionals know about what important practical steps should be taken in their decision making which are according to their basic virtues and goals. So professional ethics, whatever theoretical interest it takes, it never loses sight of the practical ethics. Therefore, it is well within holistic ethics containing the theoretical and the practical adventures. Thus in professional ethics, the practical goal of professional life and the theoretical interest in analyzing virtues of professionalism are not overlooked. Airkasinen puts it nicely: "The first and the most important message of professional ethics to professional should be that they not only aim at their own goal, they are not in conflict, as they would be from some other ethical viewpoints".[7] What we should realize is that there are some values intrinsic to the professional life and the ideal of professionalism. These values are not mere subjective inputs; they are there objectively present in professional life and professional ideals. These are unavoidable, and if we fail to recognize this truth, we have to blindly follow the common saying that professionals do not have an intrinsic ideal, values and so on but they have only care for their egoistic self which are there for subjective considerations. What can be more surprising than to disregard the claim that "good health of the public" is not an intrinsic value for medical profession? Yes, "to maintain doctor's basic existence" is also important but that is not the intrinsic goal of the medical professional. In addition, one who puts this above the intrinsic goals, is not a professional doctor, he is an amateur in the true sense of the term because he does not know his service ideal. Any way, what is clear to us is that professional ethical considerations are within the mainframe of ethics and not outside it.

Nevertheless, the supporters of modifications in professional ethics have another way to justify that codes of ethics makes great sense and that through its importance we come to know about the fact that professional ethics is well within ethics. Ethicists favouring formulation of codes of ethics, like codes of business ethics, medical ethics and so on, say that these codes are testimony to ethical importance within a non-ethical field like profession. It reflects the truth that after all ethical consciousness is an important prerequisite to an ethically untrained life. One reason may be that any formal training of ethical theories or universal principles are not what is needed for formulating ethical codes for professional but ethical consciousness may be reflected anyway in these codifications. Nevertheless, how this is possible is another thing. We shall come to know about it in the next chapter. Therefore, the whole effort, as says the modernist is hopeless, is not true. There is no doubt that many professionals do not care framing these codes, do not care to follow them either and even at times are not aware of such codes. Medical professionals are often aware of such codes in whatever insufficient way by wisdom of Hypocrites but many among them forget it quickly as nonsense. I must say that such people may not be called professionals in the true sense of the term because they have no regard for the fundamental professional ideal, rights, duties and responsibilities that these codes often reflect. However, this urgency is mainly because some wise men's esoteric coterie fixes these codes and presses them as commandments so sacred to be followed, and a dangerous idea to prize or punish goes along with such things in the professional world. I think the reason for the neglect of codes is not completely without a point. Teaching or educating a professional to become ethical or moral by memorizing the codes fixed by a group of people may not be ethical either. The whole process is wrong. But if such professional codes are basically flexible in so far as they may be revised and renewed and that such codes are results of thorough and continuous *moral dialogue* among professionals, why are they not practically as well as morally valuable is not known to me. I shall come to this problem in the next chapter. Nevertheless, for now it is very important to notice that ethical codes make some sense within professional ethics because such rules may be moral cues to a qualitatively good professional life, a life pursuing the service ideal and the several morally permissible external goods. The formulation of these codes again point towards an arduous practical process in ethics in which the moral concern of professionals have been nicely portrayed. Most interesting fact is that these codes, which are often generally, accepted statements of purposes and ideals of a profession, leaves enough room for criticism and judgment for the individual professionals, and for the reason, the codes may be revised or changed to a greater or lesser degree. Whereas this process of modification needs further analysis of ethically important aspects of professional life. The whole process of such criticism is thus essentially within the periphery of ethics. We may thus have some regard for codification in ethics, accept their value in moral life and declare that an involvement in such a thing falls within ethics.

With this background, we may now demand that a modernist in ethics should realize a few things. Some of our thinking about morality should be theoretical, some should be practical, and any disregard to latter will make a moral philosophy which is not moral. It would be a tragic outcome to justify that ethics is mental gymnastics, all good to read but it has nothing to do with public life and its betterment. People after Moore who have been following him to find out a purely formalistic character of moral philosophy, completely neglected its concrete, empirical character. It is thus completely old-fashioned to believe that morality deals with categorical, absolute and unconditional judgments. That morality propounds autonomous judgments of practice; morality stresses on universalizable principles, which are purely formal and moral judgments are emotively meaningful. It is very important to notice that morality is greatly concerned with the hypothetical judgments so prevalent in a moral dialogue in practical life situations. Such judgments are meaningful not merely emotively rather; a strong descriptive meaning underlies them, which has something to do with human experience of morally relevant facts. A universal principle so called in morality does not come from nowhere or from intuitive subsumption or due to pure thinking or are inherent in our mind, rather, they are based on practical life experiences within a morally teeming biotic life. Prescriptions from these principles need not be artificially deduced by a group of people to frame rules of conduct to impose them to make people moral. The whole body of ethics consists of philosophical analysis of essential moral concepts, justifications of universal ethical principles and practical application of ethical knowledge of the public to lead a good life. We may add to this that ethics may take care of professional ideals, codes and other essential concepts for a proper critical understanding.

The importance of application of ethics and professional ethics, and their close relationship may be justified in another way. We should try to know about the value of private and public morality and the value of moral conflicts in practical private and public life. We have seen that it is a bad habit to confuse morality and moral philosophy. A confusion of morality and ethics should be carefully avoided although there is no doubt however that ethics takes great care of morality—private and public because ethics has great practical interest. When we talk of private morality in an exclusive manner, we have to first presuppose that there is a unique human disposition to act morally and we must be rest assured of the human capacity to do the opposite as well. To conceive of such dispositions and capacities no intuitive arguments are needed. They are fairly well derived truths out of a number of human voluntary actions. One example of the importance of morals in private life of man is to be aware of good and bad manners, which are the rules, conventions and habits of behaviour. The sense of manners is peculiarly private in man and individuals are capable of knowing them and about their value almost habitually not following any rules or codes. Hence, personal morality may not be an outcome of arduous rational calculation. It is here that we are reminded of the importance of intuition in morality. However, when we come to the generalization of such manners, we find that rather than intuition, a lot of justification, particularly rational ones, are needed.

Although private morals, particularly, manners need not be generalized as principles or codes. Nevertheless, people do have such a tendency. We also have a natural inclination to pass judgments about some of the human manners when it comes to social life. However, let us remember that this does not fall under philosophical ethics. In fact, judgments about private manners often do not beg a real standard and moral calculation. However, when we come to serious moral questions covering the public life, we are facing a different situation. We start feeling that there is a great role of rational analysis, rational reflection and rational criticism in public moral life. Here our intuitions may take back seat, we may be in great need of generalized principles of morality, and these may be the crucial concern of ethics. However, things are not as simple as having on the one hand private morality not needing an ethical care and public morality needing an ethical care. For one thing, the public have the individuals having private moral life, which is very important to them apart from having moral concern for the whole public life. We must make sure that what is a stark truth in public moral life about the decision taken, about the judgments passed about actions etc. is that we have far and wide "moral disagreements" or "moral conflicts". Moreover, the conflict is among the moral agents of the society, the individuals having private moral life. Is there any point in thinking that in case of a moral conflict in social life, the conflicting individuals have no separate moral considerations and reasons to display? Is there any point to imagine that they do not agree and/or disagree individually and that they have no personal reasons to offer? The whole idea about private morality within social context is wholly not conceived if we answer these questions in the affirmative. The truth is that in the scenario of public morality, with regard to disagreement about moral values, individual morality is extremely important and their reasons are worth considering. Therefore, to think about distinct types of morality, as having no relation would be a mistake. In addition, to think that private morality is bereft of reason is equally mistaken. It is not true that in public life, moral considerations amount to big arduous theoretical analysis and arguments whereas in private life they come naturally always. Let us not forget that an individual, for instance, a professional of a particular field, when facing a moral impasse in public life and has crossed swords with others regarding how to resolve it, is not at all concerned rationally about such an impasse in private real life. What is his private moral life anyway? Is it thinking and deciding about manners, family customs, family traditions, do's and don'ts only? Not at all. A concerned moral agent in an ethical impasse in practical situations and in private conditions does care about moral questions and their resolution in a way that is more rational. He or she may argue with him, justify or reject those views, which he or she has faced or is likely to face in a public debate. Hence, private and public moral concerns are closely interwoven in many ways and the role of moral reason is indubitable. However, moral reasons are not inherent dispositions, they cannot be taught or learnt, they are rather acquired capacities of individuals in social life through effective participation in the constant flux of moral experience and moral dialogues or debates. It is very important, therefore, for moral agents to think rationally in resolving moral impasse. When a moral agent does so both privately and publicly, he or she is participating in what I have been calling applying ethical knowledge. And when the concerned public participants is engaged in a lively moral dialogue to resolve disagreements to come to a moral agreement about morally relevant questions, the public is said to have applied their knowledge in a public atmosphere along with other concerned parties (who does the same), the professionals are said to have applied their ethical knowledge. It is clear, therefore, that private and public morality in the background of moral resolution brings together the discrete individuals having moral reasons. With this, we come to know that individuals and group of people share in what we call application of ethics. We also come to know that when such application covers specific individual or groups having specific professions, we are having ethical concern in professions. What is most crucial is to notice that in both cases, "ethics" does not signify ethical theories or norms but ethical knowledge or knowledge pertaining to moral questions of desirability, rightness and goodness. Therefore, we may conclude saying that professional ethics does make sense keeping in mind both private and public morality and it is intimately related to applied ethics, where moral conflict and moral resolution are most crucial. Finally, we may also say that both professional ethics and applied ethics are within ethics proper, where "ethics" signify moral philosophy or philosophical study of morality, which includes metaethics, normative ethics, applied ethics and professional ethics. We may now say safely that rather than treating professional ethics as a branch of applied ethics, it should be known as a branch of philosophical ethics for the number of reasons given in this chapter.

NOTES

1. The discussion of "*Primary*" and "*Secondary*" group relationship can be seen in any good sociological treatise of interpersonal relationship. Readers may refer to H.H. Titus' work *Ethics for Today*, Eurasia Publishing House (Pvt.) Ltd., New Delhi, 1965, pp. 278-280 for a simple account.
2. *Ibid.*, p. 289.
3. Airaksinen, Timo, "Professional Ethics," in Ruth Chadwick (ed.) Academic Press, San Diego, 1988. *Encyclopedia of Applied Ethics* Vol. 3, p. 678.
4. Readers may go through interesting definitions of "*Profession*" revealing the important factors mentioned by me provided by Professor Cart. F. Trench in "Profession and Business Ethics", NY, Henry Holt & Co., 1926 and by Morish Logan in "The problem of defining a profession", *The Annals of the American Academy of Political & Social Science*, CCXCVII, Jan. 1983, pp. 105-111.
5. Airaksinen, Timo, "Professional Ethics" in Ruth Chadwick (ed.) *Encyclopedia of Applied Ethics*, Vol. 3, *op. cit.* p. 671.
6. For more details, readers may go through John Kultgen's *Ethics and Professionalism*. University of Pennsylvania, Pennsylvania, 1988.
7. Airaksinen, Timo, *op. cit.*, p. 674.

3

On Models of Applying Ethics

Modern moral philosophy has been doing a little too much with both metaethics and normative ethics. However, strong voice of protest has been heard now and then. Many moral thinkers raised anti-theory slogan, which includes a protest against an artificial application of normative theories in practical resolutions of moral impasse. Some people like Michael Stocker think that this over doing with "theory" has been a "schizophrenic malady". Other moral thinkers, who find it repugnant to relegate ethics to metaethics, have argued at length that without normative discussion or theoretical discussion about moral standards, ethics makes no sense. However, few moral thinkers have shown more seriousness about the problem of method in ethical application. In recent times, we do find ethicists caring for methods of ethical application for they now know that much confusion about applying ethics is owing to vagueness of methods of ethical application. Here it is interesting to notice that such confusion shroud the minds of ethical skeptics and the overdoing ethical theorists. In fact, skeptics' confusion may be largely due to the confusion created by the overdoing theorists. Therefore, the troubleshooters for applied ethics are no doubt the ethical skeptics but they have been indirectly helped by the pure theorists because it is they who had invoked the propaganda that ethical application is "application of normative ethical theories" by ethics experts to resolve a value-laden case of practical urgency. Naturally, the skeptics would raise eyebrows and argue that such things do not and need not happen. They end up in saying that therefore, applying ethics is a trash and it is not within ethics proper. We have to defend the case of applied ethics by showing the misconception about the methods of application of ethics nurtured by the pure theorists and the skeptics. Further, we have to justify what should be the proper methodology of ethical application. This is the most important task for all of us who take interest in applying ethics. All beginners have to know about it as well.

To start the discussion we have to first consider some confusion of the ethical skeptics and show why such confusions are about method of ethical application. Rhus Rhees in "Some development in Wittgenstein's view of ethics" in Philosophical Review (p. 23, 1965)[1] reports that when he once asked Wittgenstein about resolving the practical moral confusion faced by a person to make a choice between getting married and choosing a research career in cancer, Wittgenstein replied, "this question does not make sense".[2] Why does it not make sense? Wittgenstein was of the opinion that it is so because the resolution of such a moral dilemma for a person would beg the rightness of a presupposition of either Christian ethics or Nietzsche's ethics or whatever standard you call upon. Therefore, a normative theory, its correctness has to precede such resolution, and it will be very difficult to ascertain which theory is the correct one and why only that theory ought to be applied by the person. Therefore, he says, "It must be possible to decide which of the two standards of accuracy the right one is. We do not even know what a person who asks this question is after".[3] Wittgenstein was clearly speaking about the apparent confusion in deciding between normative theories in resolving practical value-laden questions, which is so common to almost all pluralists (we have discussed them). It is clear, therefore, that the confusion about practical moral resolution is confusion about method of resolution of application. Here, the method is taken to be an artificial application of any one moral theory, which is understood to be true. Nevertheless, why one theory is true is not known to Wittgenstein and to the pluralist. Although one thing is known to be true, i.e., only "ethical pluralism" as a normative standard holds good. Is it not queer? Whatever it may be, one thing we fail to understand is why at all these skeptics should imagine that ethical application amounts to application of ethical theories by an ethicist. This may be due to the pervading schizophrenic malady among the skeptics and the pure theorists.

Moreover in such cases of dilemma (personal or interpersonal), we tend to forget that often choosing between options in a situation of dilemma calls for considering the nature of alternatives to be chosen. The question is, are the alternatives equally compatible or incompatible? If they are not equally compatible, the question of moral choice is hopeless, and the one before the bachelor scientist was almost like this. Therefore, he was facing no moral dilemma at all for resolution through applying his knowledge of ethical theories. If the case is inter-personal or before a large groups of people, even then the question of compatibility cannot be overlooked. Even if the case of dilemma is perfectly compatible, the moral resolution need not beg the acceptance of choosing a theory among plurality of theories because that would amount to accept that, given this socio-economic, political etc. situations, we have to accept "this theory to be true" and then apply it to resolve the moral impasse. I have argued earlier that one who does not accept inherent pluralism in moral opinion in society, i.e., the truism of rational moral disagreement, there can be no rational moral agreement within groups of people in the society either. Therefore, there is no possibility of absolutism within pluralism for ethical application. Further, we forget that ethical application (in case of dilemma between perfectly compatible ethical alternatives) is taken to be theory-based manipulation by expert people. Therefore, the old notion of artificial ethical application is the main troubleshooter.

Let us now come to some contemporary ethical skeptics, Western and Indian. First, we have to understand that contemporary ethical skeptics generally do not ask old-fashioned questions like, "who has the moral authority to apply ethical theories?" Rather they ask, "What it is to apply ethical theories?" Because they think that "application of ethical theories" is in itself a vague expression, the meaning of it is not clear. They ask, "which ethical theories are said to be applied, metaethical or normative or both? Next they ask, "If normative ethical theories are said to be applied, how the application can take place when it is contrary to our experience, that in a situation of moral crises, no one really applies a theory?" The first question reminds us of what we have called, "schizophrenic malady" whereas the second one is most important, i.e., about proper "method" of ethical application. However, if the first question is not addressed properly, the second question remains unanswered. Therefore, the "schizophrenic malady" has to be tackled first.

Edgar Morscher, Otto Neumaier and Peter Simmons edited, "*Applied Ethics in a Troubled World*" (Kluwer, 1998) wrote a beautiful introduction on Applying Ethics in which the schizophrenic trouble has come up. The editors, clearly influenced by the writings of Morscher[4] tell us "we shall outline a simple model for applied ethics, so understood".[5] And the way it has to be understood is, "what is applied in Applied Ethics is ethics itself, more precisely, prescriptive or normative ethics, in the sense of the theory or a theoretical enterprise. There is no single prescriptive ethics: what there is instead is a plethora of different theories or attempts at theories in prescriptive ethics. Whenever such an ethical theory or part or a principle from one, is employed with regard to a concrete case or used to solve a moral problem, one is applying ethics".[6] The editors go on citing an example to make things more clear—"One is doing applied ethics when for example applying principles of utilitarian moral theory to perform about traffic speed limits or atomic power stations. One is doing applied ethics when using the categorical imperative to justify why a doctor may not lie to a mortally ill patient about his or her condition. One is doing applied ethics when using Roman Catholic moral teaching to justify forbidding euthanasia or abortion"[7]. It is clear that the editors have no doubt about ethical application being "application of ethical theories" like utilitarianism (of course not emotivism) to value-laden cases of moral urgency. Then they help the ethicists to make them believe that the method of applying ethics is, "when a moral conflict situation becomes apparent as such, or when we confront a moral problem, we look around for moral principles. Occasionally we conversely look around for situations, which are cases of the moral principles so that they can be taken to test the moral principle we have the kind."[8] This is unique. Either we look around for "normative theories" or "we conversely look around for situations" or "we may look around for both" because when we look around for normative theories we have to further look around for situations to apply them (in case of perfectly morally compatible ones) and when we look around for situations, we further look around for theories. Most interesting thing is to notice that the editors like many writers and editors of a book of applied ethics goes on picking up such situations one by one and speaks about theoretical resolutions or picks up situations and selects a moral theory to resolve moral dilemmas.

It is interesting here to see what our Indian skeptics has to say. Let me clarify here that the case of our editors was not one of the skeptics because they have hardly any doubt about applying ethics. Their case is the one of pure theorists who would extend a helping hand to ethical skeptics. Indian skeptical thinking is a good example to understand this. In India, where we are beginners in this field, we may not have many such examples. I have picked up the cases of Dr. Rajendra Prasad and Dr. S.K. Ookerjee from what I found in their papers published in the *Journal of the Indian Council of Philosophical Research*, and to which I reacted by writing a sequel of essays in the same journal.[9] Prasad writes, "in a tricky situation one may fail to see how the relevant theory or theories are to be applied"[10] and Ookerjee adds, "This entire idea of applying moral knowledge or moral principle is misconceived. In normal cases, people do, of course, act morally, but they do not do so by applying available ethical knowledge".[11] Both Prasad and Ookerjee are heavily influenced by ethical theorists, as it appears because they have no doubt about the fact that ethical application is application of a normative theory and the method is "looking around for theories and/or situations". So what is the conclusion? Ookerjee is more emphatic in his skepticism as far as he rejects applying ethics as hopeless venture within ethics. More interestingly, he does so by making it clear that "moral knowledge" and "moral principle" are one and the same thing (his use of "or"). We shall come to it later on.

It is time now that we face these theorists' confusions and skeptics' challenge. To do so, first we have to show why applying ethics is not "looking around type of method". This will take us to the other task, i.e., to show that ethics is not "applying any one or more ethical theories or principles or ethical knowledge". In order to perform the first task (a negative one) the best way is to consider some such "looking around methods" and analyze them for their inherent defects. We may call these methods "deductive and inductive methods". The more popular one, that is, the "deductive method" consists of a number of sub-methods, each coming together to fall in one cluster owing to their basic family resemblance. To name a few, we have the 'fruits-of-the-theory', the 'engineering', the 'principlist', the 'reflective equilibrial' and the 'conventional' models of ethical application. On the other hand, the inductive model does not show much variance. Therefore, it has to be discussed separately. Among the deductive models, the 'fruits-of-the-theory' and the 'engineering' models need a more careful treatment for they are old-hat, initiators of the debate and more or less influencing the latter types.

However, before we move on to the types of ethical deductivism, we should first know why we call this method "deductive". "The answer is simple", says our editors, and goes on, "the application of moral principles and ethical theories to concrete situations, problems, conflicts etc. is nothing else but the application of a covering principle (generalizing from the term 'covering law') using what we may call subsumptive inference. From a given moral principle and a series of instances of the antecedent conditions, sentences that are empirically verifiable, we may infer the corresponding instantiation of the prescriptive consequence."[12] To be clearer, first let us consider a true moral principle, then move on to a moral situation, speak of conditions and draw conclusions, which are resolutions of moral dilemma. This is applying ethics. Therefore, what we do is that we deduce prescriptions (moral acts, moral decisions and moral choice) in the face of moral dilemma from a true, established moral principle, which we think suits best in such resolution. For instance, in case of applying utilitarianism to resolve the case of capital punishment to a child abuser, we may imagine a deductive model as follows:

(1) We ought to maximize general happiness for the maximum population.
(2) Legally decided capital punishment is desirable in some cases to extend maximum happiness to maximum people.
(3) Child abuser is the one against such maximization of general happiness.

Therefore, we ought to extend capital punishment in such cases of child abuser.

The problem is do we think that moral deduction of this kind is what is applying ethics? It is better to drop general criticism of deductivism and take up the kinds of deductivism one by one. Let us start with the fruits-of-the-theory-model. Professor J.M. Brown has mentioned about this model in his essay "On applying ethics" in J.D.G. Evans edited, "*Moral Philosophy and Contemporary Problems*".[13] The 'fruits-of-the-theory model' is very simple. It is based on a strong presupposition that if we want to speak about "applying ethics", it has to rest on a well justified general ethical principle; a careful deduction of what follows from such a principle, i.e., what sort of moral prescription follows from it; a careful analysis of whether in a real life situation, the prescription would be useful in resolving a moral crises and the adoption of the prescriptive guideline as a paradigm in moral resolution and moral decision, i.e., application of the fruits of an ethical principle in a way that it becomes fruitful in practical cases. This is essentially deductive model that proceeds from the 'top to down' or that this is an abstract philosophical theorizing with the help of a so-called well justified ethical principle prescribing rules of actions and then fitting these rules in order to know what to do and what not to do in a particular situation of moral dilemma.

Several questions arise here. One is that, why should we think that an ethical theory is the soundest one in resolving all moral dilemmas? Ethical theory is so open-ended that one does not know what comes next and where it stops. In an ever evolving society, moral crises is continually emerging and with the diversity of the nature of such crises, one is not sure that one body of sound ethical theory is potent enough to resolve all of them because this is a matter of evidential inquiry and not a matter of intuition. No amount of theorizing can help us to know that a particular theory is helpful in resolving all moral dilemmas. Hence, looking around from the top will not help us in a moral resolution.

Moreover, is it possible to enlist all the fruits of an ethical theory? When we are engaged in establishing an ethical theory and telling what it consists of, and when we are engaged in a metaethical effort to justify a theory, we really do not start enlisting the fruits of the theory instantly. It is a matter of theoretical interest, which comes in due course to our realization that the theory so framed has a practical value because several moral impasses may be resolved based on what follows from that theory. In fact, there is always urgency in establishing a moral theory. This is to frame a standard of moral judgment and moral decision-making. As such, it is not odd to suppose that based on an ethical theory we may draw some such suggestions or prescriptions in the form of action-guiding and decision-making rules, which may be of practical value. However, it is odd to think that the prescriptions may be deduced in very strict logical sense. Hence, prescriptions may be said to be matter of *heuristic understanding* and not a matter of deduction following strict rules. We cannot say, for instance, that utilitarianism is a moral theory from which it may be logically deduced that "we ought to help the poor" or that "child rapist and murderer should be given capital punishment" because these rules or prescriptions may be heuristically understood to follow from the first principle (which may be debated for there may be disagreement) but it should not be taken as a conclusion that follows necessarily from the premises stated above. The heuristic understanding of what the "fruits-of-the-theory" may be is a continuous process of understanding. It does not depend on "from-the-top" deduction. This has been made aptly clear by Mill himself when he calls these heuristic rules as the "secondary rules" of morality but there may be serious disagreement about these rules, and then one has to take recourse to the first principle.

Again, it is worth asking that even if the prescriptions are heuristically understood to follow from a general ethical principle, is it useful in resolving a moral impasse. The question really cannot be unequivocally answered following pure philosophical theorizing because it calls for a serious involvement in resolving a moral trifle, which is essentially practical in nature. To delve into it is to delve into the actual cases of moral crises and finding ways to move out of them. It is in this context that we can address ourselves to the question asked above. How can we really know that the fruits of such and such ethical theory do help in resolving a moral impasse if we do not have the experience of a moral problem the resolution of which, fundamentally reflects the basic involvement of an ethical theory? That an ethical theory is not simply the handmaid of ethical theorizing is a matter of discovery through moral experience. This is not to reject ethical theorizing because we may sensibly theorize about the application possibilities of a theory and about the prescriptions likely to follow from them but such speculative enterprise will have a value if and only if we relate it to real life affairs. Ethical theorizing like this might have social value because it is of theoretical or academic interest for the philosophers but if it is in isolation, divorced from the actual contexts of application; it has no practical value. From all this we may conclude that the "fruits-of-the-theory", model in applied ethics turns out to be a model useful for exclusive ethical theorizing in which philosophers may participate in enthusiastic speculation. It conceives of ethics experts who can apply the fruits of a theory successfully. This is to avoid the non-philosophers in ethical application because they have no knowledge of ethical theories and they lack in speculation of the prescription and in applying them to resolve moral crises. Even if we accept this peculiar division of labour in ethical application, some doubt remains whether or not even philosophers can really do what they are really expected to do. Ethical application in a deductive way—"from the top", is very absurd. This absurdity in a much intense form can be seen in the "engineering model" or the "dominant conception" of applying ethics.[14]

One final point before we proceed to consider the "engineering model". The theorists influenced by deductivism, particularly influence the skeptics in order to nurture a misconception about applied ethics which is very clear. What is not clear is that why do skeptics wrongly understand that normative theories are applied in cases of moral dilemma by virtue of logically deducing the fruits of the normative theories. One good example to understand how fruits-of-the-theory model has influenced Indian thinkers, particularly the ethical skeptics, is to go through what Professor Prasad and Professor Ookerjee (P-O henceforth) says. Prasad thinks that ethical theories that may be applied are "norms, principles, criteria of rightness"[15] and S.K. Ookerjee take them to be "something like the Ten Commandments or good parental advice or copy book maxims."[16] However, Ookerjee says that even if ethical theories are just these things, it can hardly be said to be applied by people in real-life situation. First, ethical theories are generalized principles in morality, believed to act as the standard of moral judgments, as ideals, intrinsically valuable and thus worth desirable. They are the guiding force of moral actions and potential sources of moral choice and moral decision. However, these theories are known to people possessing a highly technical knowledge. The problem is how could Prasad mean moral theories to be the same as what Ookerjee interprets them to be? I do not think Prasad could mean that (neither should Ookerjee) because ethical first principles and the secondary moral rules are not the same thing. Prasad is correct in thinking that moral principles or the final principles of morality (Ookerjee calls them "super principles") are the basic norms, which ought to be followed for their intrinsic worth. They are thus the criteria of rightness as well. However, secondary rules or principles are like the "sign posts", says J.S. Mills in "Utilitarianism" which does not follow logically from the first principle but are the moral cues in following the end principle. These secondary principles are like the commandments, pieces of parental advice, social maxims etc. Hence, these principles cannot be the same as the generalized principles of morality. However, the tragedy is that there may not be a single general moral principle, which can fit into all changing moral situations. Hence, anyone general principle in morality might not resolve all moral problems nor can it guide moral actions in all changing situations in real life. This may end up in moral relativism or pluralism, which encourages skepticism of another kind because one may think that in fact, it is hopeless to speak about normative ethical theories. This would result in the rejection of normative ethics, and with this, exclusive attachment to metaethics in ethics may be encouraged. (We have already discussed the defects of such a position). Prasad and Ookerjee were careful not to run into this rough weather but if they stick too much to their view that a normative ethical theory is expected to resolve all moral crises, they are in danger. Why should there be one moral theory, which is absolutely and logically so sound that it can resolve all moral problems? Why should skeptics think that in the absence of one sound theory or ethical theories morality is in no case applied? Finally, why should we think that normative ethical theories are a bunch of theories, completely known to us (as if there can be no more), and we can choose one according to its merit and then fit it to a situation to resolve a moral problem? Yes, I agree with Prof. Ookerjee when he says, "recalling a relevant principle, applying it, deciding to act on it and then acting on it all this just does not happen".[17] But to say that therefore, applying ethics is an enigma is incorrect. This skeptical confusion (P-O type) leads to dangerous propositions like the conception of "wise, ethics experts" or "Plato's guardians" according to Prasad. This is naturally the climax of ethical engineering, to which we shall concentrate soon. Such moral engineers may possess "cultivated moral sense", says Prasad, which is "partly inherited". Hence, we may imagine hereditary moral sense transmitting from one generation to the other as per the Phaedogenetics of Plato (this is, migrating souls carry moral knowledge as well as other dispositions). This Prasad would not accept I believe, or will he accept it? Let us leave it here and now move on to the "engineering model" to discover more things that are interesting.

This model is related to the fruits-of-the-theory model as far as it propagated the idea that there is one body of ethical theory which can be rightly chosen by an ethics expert to engineer moral problems. Not only this, the experts has to engage in a teaching programme of ethical theory or theories (almost undertaking it as an art) which will educate non-philosophers about how to apply one theory or the other as the situation demands. The model has been well elucidated by Arthur Caplan and Alasdair McIntyre who, however, terms it as the "dominant conception" of moral resolution[18]. More than that, the engineering model finds support directly or indirectly from many fashionable writers of applied ethics. What Caplan explains in terms of "ethical engineering", is a "deductive model" because here a well established ethical theory is conceived as a successful tool in moral engineering, i.e., for deriving a set of practical recommendation or trying them to apply to resolve the cases of moral impasse. Why this is called "moral engineering", is clear to us. It speaks of an ethics expert, who has an encyclopedic knowledge of ethical theories, their nuances and relative merits and demerits (and more peculiarly, knows why one or the other theory is perfectly suitable for moral resolution). The expert or the engineer is further supplied moral problems by non-philosophers and other concerned parties, who then displays his engineering by virtue of pressing the right theory (tool) from his knowledge repository (tool box) to mend moral defects (practical value-laden problems). Thus the specific steps in moral engineering are: choosing the right ethical theory to be applied, analyzing the value-laden problem supplied by the non-philosophers, clearly enlisting the practical recommendations that follow from an ethical theory chosen for moral resolution, then solving the value-laden problem and finally, taking up a teaching task of theoretical ethics keeping in mind the poor non-philosophers so that they become ethical engineers in near future.

With this, the division of labour and monopolistic chauvinism of ethicists spelt out in this model haunt our minds. These peculiar people called "philosophers" sit high in their ivory towers of ideals with their kits full of ethical knowledge, awaiting the professionals of different fields, the non-philosopher-cry-babies to supply moral problems and await ethical engineers to prescribe a list of duties as well as ethics teaching. Such vanguards of ethics thus apply a well-grounded general ethical theory in order to resolve moral crises in different professional fields like medicine, agriculture and many more. Hence, ethical issues that arose in a profession do not become a genuine problem for a professional in the sense that they are not supposed to get involved in resolving that problem, i.e., they do not become a party to that effort. Professional ethical problems are thus problems for the ethics experts to resolve.

Given this version of ethical engineering, which is a gross form of being influenced by the "schizophrenic malady", the P-O type confusion will naturally arise. However, once we understand that this is not applied ethics such confusions are dispelled. This model of ethical application bears the seventeenth century tendency to give ethical guidance to the society, which is popularly known as *casuistry*. Moreover, casuistry is quite capable of bewildering the best minds to believe that this is what applied ethics is. In fact, skeptics' confusion is largely owing to the confusion that applied ethics is casuistry. Even W.K. Frankena has no doubt about it. He writes in his book "Ethics", "Today some philosophers seek to do something like this (casuistry) by discussing the ethics of abortion… and war… In doing so, however, they characteristically tend, rightly in my opinion, to stress *general principles*. This is a most philosophers as such can be expected to do, and it can be very helpful."[18] This "from the top" resolution of ethical problems by an expert turns out to be a linear application of a moral theory by an ethicist, as if it were an "art". If one suffers from these confusions one fails to know what applied ethics really is. Moreover, as was expected, our editors (Morscher *et al.*) in their introduction in page xviii put a heading: "The State of the Art of Applied Ethics". However, what is this "art"? Who teaches the rules? If applied ethics is an art, as is casuistry, we may enter into *sophistry* unknowingly.

Let us now understand the difference between casuistry and applied ethics. Casuistry, like sophistry, takes the form of providing moral agents facing conflict among duties, with an intelligible set of moral reasoning to resolve such conflicts. Hence, it is sometimes referred to as an "art of moral resolution", whereas applied ethics is not an art (specialized by ethicists) of applying one sound-body of ethical theory in order to resolve all value-laden problems. There can be really no art of ethics, which can help a moral agent in moral reasoning by producing a set of universally true moral rules or moral prescriptions. (We have discussed this as well.) The most sincere effort to teach application of ethical theories in order to make people ethical has to fail miserably because one cannot act like an artist to perfect the moral practices of people and that too with the help of a sound ethical theory. The problem is that an ethicist, if he is crafty enough to call his ethical knowledge into service to find ways out of moral trifles, can fail miserably in his art in many other demanding situations. Sometimes there will be poverty of ideas, sometimes obsession with one theory will mislead him or her and sometimes he or she will fail to understand the gravity of a problem and to find ways to resolve it with the help of a given tool in his toolbox. The moral engineers or the casuists, a miserable lot, suffer from all orthodoxy that there could be in ethical theorizing and ethical application.

What is nauseating in the engineering model is that non-philosophers have no moral confidence in applying ethics because they do not have the so-called "moral knowledge" (or to Prasad, the "knowledge of ethical theories"). A philosopher then has to enter into moral affairs of different occupations to help professionals. Is this an acceptable situation? No perhaps. First, non-philosophers need not "supply" moral problems to ethics experts. No doubt, ethicist cannot be omnipotent information gatherers from all occupations and professions. He has to rely on other professionals in this regard. However, that does not mean that professionals supply ethical problems to ethicists. Rather, the professionals have the first hand experience of such moral trifles. However, that does not prevent them from having an interdisciplinary interest. I must say that an understanding of whether or not a practical problem is value-laden is not the sole business of an ethicist. A practical problem figuring in a particular field does not become value-laden when ethicists say so. Whether or not it is value-laden, we all know from our ethical experience. In an applied ethics discourse there is thus no division of labour like non-philosophers doing one thing and ethicists doing the rest. That a problem raises ethical questions of serious concern is a matter of plain ethical experience that we all have in the society we live in and we all have a moral viewpoint as well as moral authority to solve moral problems. The truth we strike at now is that applied ethics is not moral engineering. The deductive model is to be discarded anyway.

I think we had enough about knowing the inherent defects in the "deductive models". Once we keep these things in mind, deductive models may be understood as, "dominant conception" of morality suggested by Sidgwick, Rawls and Brandt. Moral theories are looked upon by these thinkers as some such abstractions, which categorize moral agents, their actions and outcomes into appropriate categories. Different moral theories consider different categories as primary. For instance, utilitarianism takes "value of consequence of actions" as primary whereas deontology takes "value of infatuation free duty" as primary. Another point is that these universal moral theories have an implicit coercive force, which binds the moral agent to a moral decision followed by an action. The task of a moral thinker is to analyze both the universal character of a moral theory and the coercive power inherent in it so that a moral agent may practically apply them in situations to morally decide, act and resolve moral impasse. It is due to this fact that a moral theory does not remain a handmaid of theoretical analysis rather, becomes a "tool" for moral resolution. For this we have to imagine on the one hand ethicists who are engaged in a theoretical churning and further teaching the more or less ethics—less mass about the universalized moral theories. Maybe the ethicists has to show which theory fits into which situations. When all this is done by the expert, the non-ethicists, who have supplied a moral problem to the ethicist, apply a theory to find out what are the do's and don'ts in a particular situation. The moral engineering is thus clear and it is needless to repeat all the defects troubling the engineering model. Nevertheless, we may point out here that a large number of ethicists have been influenced by a more feminine model of ethical application rather than the above-mentioned patriarchic model because the "feminine model" propagates an empathetic involvement of moral thinkers with other parties for moral resolution and not simply acting vanguards of ethical application. The reason is that the application of ethics in itself has been viewed as a moral practice, essentially Aristotelian in spirit rather than Kantian or is unlike any other deductivists or even unlike the church fathers, the casuists or the older sophists. It is due to this that in the application of ethics, we have "from bottom down" approach rather than the "from the top" approach. What the critiques of the "deductive" or the "dominant conception" have in mind is that an ethical theory may fail miserably in the face of artificial resolution of moral problems by an expert for the obvious reason that an ethical theory does not enjoy that absolutist authority. The reason is simple. Moral trifles are largely our cultural problems, which rather than finding solutions through ethical theories gives way to informed disagreements. Therefore, we can hardly have ethical theories by themselves mending moral defects particularly within the social context. All interested parties in moral resolution may not come together to accept one ethical theory to be correct and suitable for moral resolution. Therefore, in the social milieu of moral disagreement, ethical theories fail to deliver what we expect from them. G.E.M. Anscombe, Alasdair McIntyre and Bernard Williams thus take an extreme "anti-theory" stand to reject deductivism of all sorts, which takes us to consider the relationship between moral theory and moral practice *de novo*. Dale Jameson in his article in Peter Singer edited, "A Companion to Ethics" (p. 480) writes "the anti-theorists reminds us that people in their everyday moral practices create theory, that there are limits on what these theories can do; that their job is to help us do what is right rather than to be true....however, what they did not succeed in showing is that we would be better off without moral theory"[19]. There is some truth in what Jameson says, particularly when he evaluates the position of this extreme antitheorist stance. However, we shall come to it after I have propounded my position regarding this matter.

However, for the time being let us consider some other deductive models of ethical application, which need not be analyzed in great details because we have had enough of this model so far. In the field of bioethics some thinkers came together to suggest that by avoiding ethical pluralism in the context of interpersonal moral dialogue, and by avoiding ethical absolutism in the older deductivist trend, we may conceive of a *mid-level theory* composed of three basic principles of autonomy, beneficence and justice. This theory, claims its supporters viz., Tom Beauchamp and James Childress ("Principles of Biomedical Ethics") that the principles are in fact inherent some way or other in our basic traditions of normative ethical theory, which have a unique capacity to guide practical moral judgement (at least in medicine). The supporters say that this model of "principlism" overcomes the problems of abstraction as well as artificial application by mingling the basics of general ethical theory and their inherent applicative capacity. Nevertheless, the crux of the problem is that 'principlism' does involve the problems of abstracting three basic principles from among ethical theories and does have the problem that such a high-level theoretical work, akin to deducing truths from a body of available information and subsequent application in fields like medicine demands ethical expertise. Therefore, deductivism and engineering both are very much there. We have seen just now that such deduction of principles and applying them in practical cases may be as impossible as was the case with the early deductivists or the supporter of the 'dominant conception'. Earl R. Winkler remarks in an essay entitled: "Applied Ethics, Overview" (*Encyclopaedia of Applied Ethics*, Volume 7, p. 193), "the same problem of a historicism and abstraction reappearing with the standard mid-level normative theories, in bioethics and elsewhere".[20] The real problem is that against the excessive theorists' jugglery in deductivism, the so-called universalized ethical theories have crystallized through unnatural abstraction in a manner so that the historical realities, sociological realities, traditions, cultures and even moral experiences have been grossly overlooked. Once we expect a little too much with these ethical theories in decision making and action guiding, overlooking the real life factors, ethical theories turn out to be useless. This is what I have got from practical experience in applying ethics. Yet, I will not take an extreme view, as did Williams and many anti-theorists that ethical theories have no role to play in ethical application. We shall come to it later on.

However, let us not expect that I am extending a support to the more refined version of ethical application called the model of "reflective equilibrium" which tends to find equilibrium between deductivism based on ethical theories and real life involvement in moral resolution where individual's moral disagreement rule supreme (including the free interplay of historical, social and cultural factors). The very conception of the model of "reflective equilibrium" is based on another unnatural dialectical fine tuning between our moral evaluations about concrete case in the context of historical, cultural changes and our commitment to principle, or better say, our commitment to the fact that general ethical principles after all shall override our moral evaluation in deducing working ethical principles. This fine-tuning or finding equilibrium is another old-hat because the old deductivistic tendency is still alive in it. Deriving ethical principles from overriding general theories by ethics experts to obtain moral tools or social instruments to apply in different domains of social life is lurking in it. No doubt, here the historicism and moral experiences of the public are kept in mind; the overriding ethical theoreticism is nonetheless most prominent. It is due to this that Winkler remarks: "there seems to be no good reason to assume that all defensible moral standards will be explicable in terms of a deductive relationship to some more or less determinate normative context. Although such a theoretical reduction or reconstruction may be possible, in spite of cultural diversity and in spite of the overwhelming failure of all previous efforts to gain general acceptance of any set of fundamental moral principles, many now regard this enterprise as exceedingly doubtful, even philosophically naive".[21] Whatever it may be, I would still not relegate ethical generalization to be valueless in ethical application. This will be justified at a proper place.

Again there is no need to think that I am hinting towards the more recent model of professional consultancy in which ethicists within defined institutional setting participate in some kind of interpersonal dialogue with professionals of diverge fields to know about their moral dilemma, talk to them about their professional virtues, take suggestions, discuss and decide "what to do when". This is happening around us particularly in the business schools. I have seen the Indian Institute of Management in Calcutta inviting people to apply for a teaching post in the Department of Human Values demanding that apart from other tasks, the person has to undertake a "consultancy task" within the defined institutional settings. This is happening more widely in different government commissions, committees, and organizations and even in hospitals and courts. Nevertheless, what is new in it? Is it not the same ethical expertise, the same overriding misconception that these experts have the knowledge of ethical theories and professional virtues to evaluate moral decisions and resolve moral impasse? Clearly, if moral resolution and decision-making were dependent on knowledge of general principle and apply it to cases in a predominantly artificial way then, the ethical experts, who are skilled in moral engineering, would be necessary. This would need a lot of training both on the part of the consultant ethicist as well as on the part of those prospective professionals in different fields who want to be ethics experts as well. The training would involve normative ethics as well as metaethics, and if we have a chance to tackle the moral problems faced by a worker in a business organization, how our ethics experts resolve their trifles by mere sophistical dialogue will be interesting to notice. Further how would a worker of an organization be trained of his professional values and norms of ethics for ethical application will be more interesting to notice. Hence, ethical expertise demands some such things, which are not different from ethical engineering. We may thus carefully avoid all forms of ethical deductivism with a caution, however, that there may be enough reasons not to discard general ethical theories from the process of ethical application.

Let us now come to the *inductive* or the "from-the-bottom model" of ethical application. This is sometimes popularly known as "contextualistic model", which is worth analyzing before I move on to the model supported by me. I must mention that I have certain reservations about this so-called anti-theorists' pet model but the model has something in it which is worth commending. A proper evaluation of the inductive or the contextualistic model is possible if we now clearly point out the position of the anti-theorists or the anti-deductivists (remember I am speaking of the more radical ones and I am not including myself in this group). Anti-theorists hold that: (a) deductivists are wrong in preoccupied with highly abstract universal rules and principles, when our intuition basically show any favour towards one theory for all moral resolutions; (b) deductivists are extreme reductionists and wrongly argues that all moral values can be thought of under one monistic principle, and (c) deductivists are wrong in assuming that moral reasoning is only deductive in nature because for every moral problem there is a correct decision emanating from a overriding theory through a reductive procedure.

Anti-theorists argue that: (a) moral resolution through application of ethics is generated not through artificial application of standard ethical theories but considering particularities of actual cases and situations; (b) moral resolution demands not merely ethicists but all concerned parties to apply their available ethical knowledge, which is 'uncodified' or not the same as (what Prasad thinks) knowledge of standard ethical theories; (c) hence, moral resolution needs precedence of moral experience, which is not intuitive experience of a codified moral principle rather experience stemming out of our moral activities in the ecological community; (d) the set of historical, sociological, cultural, empirical, logical elements involved in actual cases or contexts of moral conflicts have to be seriously considered for an interpersonal moral dialogue; (e) in doing so ethical theories may be created and known but they need not become axioms of further deduction; and (f) moral resolution through interpersonal contextual evaluation of moral trifles helps in filtering out a relative set of moral cues in professional decision making.

The above position is called 'contextualistic' as far as the real life cases of moral conflicts are considered for moral resolution keeping in mind the conventions, traditions and historical and local explanations. The model is called 'inductive' not because it is a logical corollary of the deductive model rather owing to the fact that *instances* of moral crises are considered as initiating point of theoretical analysis within the historical and local explanations followed by a satisfactory resolution by a well-moderated moral dialogue *if needed.* This may further create ethical theories of secondary importance nevertheless the model is thus 'from the bottom' because primary importance has been given to the basic fact in moral application, which is, application of the moral knowledge of the concerned parties, the knowledge which is 'uncodified'. The model thus puts much stress to the non-philosophers' and philosophers' basic ability to participate in an able analysis of moral problems and their resolution. J.C. Callahan who is a celebrated name in the field of applied ethics and has cared for the questions of methodology in ethical application, has put the spirit of contextual ethical application before the ethical skeptics saying, "Although applied ethics borrow insight from theories of moral axiology, theories of moral obligation and metaethics, the task in engaging in practical ethics is not simply to work out application of existing ethical theories. It is rather to attempt to find acceptable resolutions of moral problem of present and practical urgency. This involves much more than merely doing some sort of philosophical technology where high level theory is simply brought over to practice."[22] He further elaborates on what exactly this 'from the bottom' model should take on. He says, "in engaging in practical ethics: (a) recognizing moral issues to start with; (b) developing the moral imagination; (c) sharpening analytical/ critical skills; (d) testing out disagreements; (e) effecting decisions and behaviour; and (f) implementation, closure and process, are of vital importance."[23]

We may, therefore, say that according to contextualism universal ethical theories are needless in resolving ethical crises. Rather, we proceed to ethical decision-making and practical resolution by considering what *ought* to be done in a particular situation. This reminds me of the Aristotelian call for our display of practical wisdom to determine mean action and thereby come out of moral trifles. However, Aristotle clearly indicated that this is only a mere means for the achievement of the higher goal, viz., eudemonia. The modern contextualists would not like to stick to an enigmatic ideal like this one and they would rather propose a shift from theoretical misadventure to our contextual free play of common ethical knowledge. Remember, this common ethical knowledge has an empirical anchor, which become most crucial in determining what generally ought to be done if such and such is the case within the given social, historical, cultural tradition. We may thus reach to obtain a *relatively justified* set of decision-making rules as well as relative justification of favouring one kind of option rather than the other in the face of moral dilemma. The whole method is thus provisional notwithstanding the value of the moral views of concerned parties and not merely that of the ethicist. Moral chauvinism is thus out of date. Nevertheless, moral disagreement and objection are open. However, our resolution has surpassed such obstacles through a *moral debate*. We may thus have at hand shared values of the public unless it is pressed hard for further moral scrutiny in changing social scenario.

One who is too worried about asking the old question of normative ethics, the contextualists say that it may be that the case-driven resolution through careful scrutiny of the pros and cons of the moral opinions may well create a theory, who knows. However, that is not an advantage. It is at this point that I would like to differ later on. Anyway, the contextualists' message is that we should be more focused in acquiring decisions appropriate to fulfilling our roles as moral agents in particular cultural and institutional situations. One advantage of this method is that we are open to the various ways of understanding and resolving moral impasse within the social context. However, unlike this method (but quite akin to it) is 'virtue ethics' which tends to see right decision as ensuing from the consideration of relevant virtues fulfilling a moral agent. This, however, is another old hat because we may soon discover that a list of virtues may assume absolute status, as were the standards of morality.

Given this contextualist turn to applied ethics, we are asking another interesting question, i.e., what should be the exact procedure through which contextual decision-making is possible? Really speaking, procedure hints at the *group moral dynamics* and decision-making. Now we have to be more clear and careful in stating what this group dynamics should be like. It is here that I would like to propose my view. Whatever it may be, we are perhaps accepting the truth that applying ethics in an inductive way calls for "free and informed consensus of all interested parties".[24] "We have at least approximated such a consensus."[25]

However, outright rejection of the deductive model does not amount to the outright rejection of moral theories. This is perhaps the worst orthodoxy in contextualism. Even if we accept that through 'approximated consensus' we have reached our deserved goal of applying our ethical knowledge, we must not forget that not only that group moral dynamics would *create* moral theories, they would most likely *reflect* some of the well known moral theories. The nagging question may be what do we do with these theories? Yes, we need not apply them as tools in ethical debate to form a consensus because even careful ethicists may fail to do so mechanically. However, we can let the interested people in ethics know that even in-group moral dynamics, ethical theories find a place. Therefore, these theories are not handmaids of our intuitive reflection, nor do we create them by our whims, these theories are constructions of our moral experience, an experience we have in this ecological community and that these theories are constructions supported by our moral arguments and rational reflection. A return to ethical theories is necessary; otherwise, the whole gamut of normative thinking will crumble to dust. Let us not forget that contextualistic model did not even care to consider this crucial point, i.e., there may be *post-consensus* theoretical work inherent in what we call applied ethics. No doubt, this may be highly restrictive to academics but we have to regard them as important, particularly when it comes to applied ethics education or teaching.

One pertinent question in the minds of the contemporary skeptics is that why do we call applied ethics a branch of ethics when there is no trace of normative and metaethics in it? If applied ethics is not artificial application of normative theories to practical value-laden cases, and it is application of our common ethical knowledge, meaning knowledge pertaining to the desirability, right, wrong, good, ought, duties and obligation, how is it within ethics? The skeptics are not to be blamed for this. They have been nurturing this confusion owing to the applied ethicists' misconception about the nature and method of applying ethics. What a number of applied ethicists have been doing all these years boils down to picking up normative theories along with a value-laden case and doing the so-called engineering. This is clear from the reports, papers, and a number of books, which have flooded the west and ripping through this country. Well, if you write a book on applied ethics informing about what are the nature and justification of different normative theories in the first part of the book and then in the second part go on to consider value-laden cases showing how one theory has the disposition to resolve it, may be it is of some help. A number of books have been written in this style. What is the benefit of going through some such books is difficult to understand. Is it not proper to return to the theory part after we have considered a real life value-laden dilemma with real people, their views, and their disagreement, their consensus (if possible), to know what views, they have adhered to or have created? Why not return to theory at this point? Our experience tells us that when you are really engaged in application of ethics in the capacity of an ethicist, you do have an important theoretical work at hand but that should come at last. Skeptics should know that this return to the theoretical work is what is unique to the trained ethicists (I will include those professionals who have been trained in ethics in this group). Therefore, neither the ethicists nor their normative theories have been dumped. It is also not that applied ethics is not within ethics in the real sense of the term and that the ethicists do not have much to do in applying ethics. Rather, ethicists do have important tasks in the application of ethics. We shall come to it when I spell out my model of ethical application. These are some important points, which the contextualist model do not take care of. A return to theory and the role of ethics and ethicists should be clearly spelt out. Another thing is that ethical application is never monolithic, it is essentially pluralistic, i.e., no one theory is often reducible when we analyze the moral debate followed by a consensus. Of course, if the participants in the debate are all conscious of a theory and its necessary application, the result is different. However, it seldom happens because you have already constructed a panel of participants each having a concern for a value-laden issue and each coming from a different profession perhaps. For instance, when you consider the case of "whistle blowing"[26] you are not expected to have only managers in your panel, you should include workers as well. Moreover, if the panel is one of the managers they may be from different organizations. If they are not from one organization, they are most unlikely to apply deontology when they talk about whistle blowing. Yet, it may be that when you talk to some socialists for instance about "computerization", they plan it or not, even if they come from different organizations, their view reflect "welfarism". Nevertheless, their arguments may be different. If you are interested in application of ethics in the fashion of a moral debate, it is better not to have theory-co-opted people. In addition, if you learn to do this, you will find that moral debates go better when you have a heterogeneous panel of theory non-coopted people. It will be very interesting as ethicists to arrange such debates, preparing value-oriented questionnaire for debates, and revise views and reasons during a dialogue, find out points of consensus, filter out the decision-making rules and then return to the theoretical ethical task. Nevertheless, if you were asked further to teach all this, you have considered another method of applied ethics teaching. I will come to this in the fifth chapter. It is now sufficient to tell that contextualistic model does leave out important points, which has to be considered now. However, not before we have met the last skeptical challenge. The skeptics may now say that all that you demand in applying ethics does speak of an ethical expertise, so the chauvinism is still there. However, the skeptics should remember that the ethicists are at best the initiators of a moral dialogue, they are one of the best persons to conduct such debates and articulate and analyze the theoretical aspects of those debates. If this be the case, where is chauvinism? Someone has to do it, is it not true? Yes, a professional of the particular field, who has been trained in ethics, may sometimes do it better by virtue of an added technical training. But then that professional who is undertaking this interdisciplinary task as is the case with the ethicists (because he should have an added technical information of problem in consideration) have moved clearly out of ethical engineering and chauvinism, for both rely on debate and consensus and not bossing from the top. Skeptics challenge that our non-philosophers turned 'ethicists' proves that at least one branch of ethics, i.e. applied ethics, is not an ethicists' affair. In addition, if that is true, applied ethics is not ethics proper for it is not done by ethicists alone. This is a little too much. Any interdisciplinary adventure has this problem of calling a name. What are biologists doing when they are engaged in some sort of engineering as well? What do we call them, a biologist, an engineer, or a nonsense group? Nothing prevents non-philosophers being trained in ethics, i.e., doctors trained in ethics, including, applying ethics and subsequently doing this application work very efficiently. If they do this, they are very much the doctors. Why attach a name to them? That does not justify them more fully as hybrid professionals. Even trained ethicists has to go through the basics of genetics for instance, to arrange a moral debate to resolve a value-laden issues in genetics. Then why do we worry to give them a new name? Both doctors and ethicists are doing sensible things within ethics. It is, therefore, that applied ethics is a group dynamics not an exclusive affair of ethics experts. Nevertheless, owing to the better ethical training, an ethicist may do this job more efficiently, particularly the job of ethical analysis of moral debates and ethics teaching. This "interdisciplinary nature" of ethical application was little subdued in the contextualist methodology. Finally, we have to satisfy the skeptic by saying that teaching wholesome ethics to these non-philosophers and informing people about the practical value of ethical theories is not a model of applying ethics, it is something else. We shall return to it when we consider the teaching methodologies.

So the stage is set for propounding my methodology of application of ethics, which I call, "intersubjective corroboration"[27]. I will start with a sweeping remark. Applied ethics is essentially a project in ethics proper that pursues interdisciplinary synthesis and construction of practical rules of moral worth to face ethical dilemma. Hence, we have to be serious about the views of different professionals to ensure a qualitative social life. A morally charged social life cannot be conceived without a morally charged public policy, and decision making rules cannot be without moral value if they do not ensure qualitative social life. Another point is that in order to resolve moral crisis and moral disagreements to construct decision-making rules and public policy, we need not (and cannot) overlook the moral view points of the public. It would be in bad taste to think of moral decision-making in collective life with an idea that non-philosophers are morally blunt even if they are morally conscious because the moral bluntness is due to their lack of the knowledge of the different ethical theories and their applications. The problem is that we have a perennial orthodoxy in our minds that philosophers have moral knowledge because "moral knowledge" is the "knowledge of the ethical theories". There is no point in having faith in such an implication because all sane, grown up humans have moral experience and have enough moral knowledge of right, wrong, ought, desirability, duty etc. This is so evident because we all participate in a society teeming with individuals engaged in intentional actions, which affect fellow beings and the biotic community adversely or favourably. We are engaged in ethical judgments, ethical scrutiny of actions and scrutiny of ends and means; we also choose and debate about our duties. We are thus in constant moral agreement and disagreement. Hence, individuals are forged in ethical experience and have ethical knowledge. These beg no teaching, all these happen without a holiday. It is absurd to think that a privileged class (ethicists) has ethical knowledge only by virtue of his unique theoretical training.

Take out moral experience and the moral knowledge in its broadest notion, the ethicists are helpless. A theory is a construction out of a theorizing process, an intellectual phenomenon essentially. It may be that intuition play a role in it, but take out individuals from the biotic community and take out the complex moral settings; any amount of intuition of an ethicist will be fruitless. Hence, the inability to construct a normative ethical theory does not hinder participating in an ethical discourse and sharing moral views. This is to look into the very "bottom" in applying our ethical knowledge to resolve moral crisis in which the philosophers are the corroborators. Intersubjective corroboration thus stands on the solid grounds of moral experience, moral knowledge and application of these things in moral crisis. One who wants to take this project seriously has to be ready to learn from others and be ready to diffuse moral hunches of others. It is corroboration of views that help in framing decision-making rules. The process is continuous and one need not think hopelessly about the vast extent of territory, of one's nation, and about the ocean of people and their views. One may be very suspicious about all this because a gang of dacoits may have ethical corroboration to act Robin Hood. The point is that a gang of dacoits does not constitute a whole nation and in case of there being one or more gangs, we need serious public policy to counter them because these gangs do not contribute to flourishing, qualitative, collective life. Ethical corroboration remains a morally valuable model in applying ethics as far as it does not become the handmaid of a group of people (philosophers or non-philosophers). If artificial application of ethical theories is not given importance, ethical corroboration is valuable. The importance and need of ethical theorizing is, however, not ruled out because there is every scope for the discovery of an interpretation of an ethical principle in the context of ethical corroboration. It is very likely that a philosopher may be careful enough to consider a context in the light of a principle. Nevertheless, this later division of labour is not all; the philosopher has to depend on a basic vocation of the social scientific model, the "intersubjective corroboration". Such corroboration of the moral views does not mean corroboration of the ethical theories. Rather, the range of ethical arguments, which reflect some of these theories, may crystallize in a dialogue to frame important decision-making rules for our professionals facing moral dilemma. It is here that applying ethics is so close to professional ethics. Nevertheless, these sets of decision-making rules are only relative, they may change, modify and fizzle out with growing disagreements, further debates and fresh consensus. Never mind, every time we have these rules, they are obtained through an essentially ethical method, where views of concerned parties have been considered. This is perfectly in tune with ethical pluralism as well. This also calls for our non-cooption with a particular theory. Thus, an ethicist, who moderates a dialogue need to be non-coopted because any artificial attempt at applying theory has to fail in the real life situation. The argument is not to forget what you know, rather, do not stick only to what you know. Do not try to boss on others based on what you know. Cooperation and consensus are more important for a qualitative democratic life. However, this is a continuous and a group work of gigantic proportion. Many concerned parties should do such things in different fields. A time comes when we do feel the need of learning the basics of ethics and ethical application. It is perhaps due to this that applying ethics has become a national creed in the UK, the USA, Australia and Canada. Why should we lag behind? It has to start somewhere following a fair sampling basis. Then it has to spread the whole nation and has to go on continuously. Nevertheless, if the government agencies are completely lackadaisical in their approach to adopt some of the decisions seriously and if professionals have no respect for them, it breaks down. Our professionals should know that their chauvinistic mentality should give way to de-classing oneself to corroborate and follow what is important for qualitative-work-life.

With this methodology at hand, I will now try to give an example of such an application of ethics with which I was engaged. Let us come to the analysis of the methodology through this example in the next chapter. This is needed because although I have said much about what involves corroboration of moral views in the context of discussing contextualism, it is time now that we know in more details about what exactly should be done under this method.

NOTES

1. Rhees, Rhus, "Some Developments in Wittgenstein's View of Ethics", *Philosophical Review*, 1965, p. 23.

2. *Ibid.*, p. 23.
3. *Ibid.*
4. Morscher, Edgar *et al.* (eds), "*Applied Ethics in a Troubled World*", Kluwer, Dordrecht, 1998, pp. ix-xxi.
5. *Ibid.*, p. ix.
6. *Ibid.*, pp. ix-x.
7. *Ibid.*, p. xiii.
8. *Ibid.*
9. Prasad, Rajendra, "Applied Ethics", *J.I.C.P.R*, Vol. xiv, No. 2, 1997, p. 3 and S.K. Ookerjee, "Rajendra Prasad – Some Comments on Applying Ethics", *J.I.C.P.R*, Vol. XV, No. 2, 1998, p. 126.
10. *Ibid.*, p. 5.
11. Ookerjee, S.K., *op. cit.*, p. 126.
12. Morscher, Edgar *et al.*, *op. cit.*, p. xiv.
13. Evans, J.D.G., (ed), *Moral Philosophy and Contemporary Problems*, Cambridge University Press, 1987, pp. 81-93.
14. Readers may refer to Arthur L. Caplan's "Mechanics on Duty: The Limitations of a Technical Definition of Moral Expertise for Work in Applied Ethics", *Canadian Journal of Philosophy*, Supplementary Volume I, 1982, pp.1-18 and Alisdair MacIntyre's essay, 'Does applied ethics rest on a mistake?' in *The Monist*, Vol. 67, No. 4, 1984, pp. 499-513.
15. Prasad, *op. cit.*, p. 10.
16. Ookerjee, *op. cit.*, p. 126.
17. *Ibid.*, p. 127.
18. Frankena, W.K., *Ethics*, Prentice Hall of India, New Delhi, 1989, p. 13.
19. Jameson, Dale, "Method and Moral Theory" in Peter Singer edited *A Companion to Ethics*, Blackwell, p. 480.
20. Winkler, Earl R., *Applied Ethics, Overview* in Encyclopedia of Applied Ethics, Vol. 7, 1998, p. 193.
21. *Ibid.*, p. 194.
22. Callahan, J.C., "Applied Ethics" in P.H. Werhane and R.E. Freeman (eds), *The Blackwell Encyclopedia of Philosophy*, Blackwell, 1997, p. 22.
23. *Ibid.*, pp. 22-26.
24. Winkler, Earl R., *op. cit.*, p. 195.
25. *Ibid.*, p. 195.
26. "*Whistle Blowing*" is a unique value-laden problem in the field of business. The problem is whether or not it is ethically desirable to raise a warning against the malpractices of a business organization even if you are a responsible manager. The moral dilemma of choice is clear—whether or not to blow the whistle or to make a piggy ride.
27. Guha, Debashis, "Intersubjective Corroboration," *J.I.C.P.R*, Vol. XIX, No. 2, 2002, pp. 43-58.

4

A Glimpse of Ethical Application through Intersubjective Corroboration

It is time now that we take a close look at the dynamics of the proposed model of ethical application. In fact what I was trying to convince is that only words do not work in ethical application, deeds work. 'To do' has been an eluding proposition through the years in applied ethics. To avoid further confusion in this matter, I have justified at length what is 'done' in applied ethics. Hence 'to do' a corroborative act along with post-corroborative analysis, is what matters in applied ethics. Following steps may be helpful:

(a) sorting out value-laden practical problems awaiting ethical resolution by interested parties, namely, the ethicists and/or the professionals of different fields;
(b) preparing a questionnaire for debates with interested parties (as many as possible), which should be so framed as to bring out the moral view points of the parties participating in the debates;
(c) arranging debates by carefully selecting the panelists, not necessarily according to their education, intellect, position etc., rather, keeping in mind whether or not the most important parties have been invited;
(d) ethicists and/or other trained professionals in ethics may act corroborators by putting these questions, inviting arguments, inciting disagreements, correcting and analyzing apparent fallacies in opinions to reach to a possible corroboration of views;

(e) collecting the points of corroboration amounting to the ethical resolution of a moral impasse by the interested parties themselves along with clear decision making rules which have been suggested by the professionals;

(f) the ethicists, or persons trained in theoretical ethics should be engaged in a further theoretical venture called, "post-corroboration analyses" of the moral debates and their findings. This consists of careful analysis of every moral opinion of the participants, preferably by taking the responses to the questions asked as they appeared serially, and then going through the closure of opinions. This would give us the effective real dynamics of ethical theories known to us or of those, which are new to us; and

(g) finally, the reflection of how a range of moral opinion found a corroborative voice to frame decision-making rules for our professionals is needed.

Let me now provide the readers a glimpse of one such ethical effort undertaken by me during 1998. For its simplicity and uniqueness, I prefer to speak about the "Ethic of Bonsai", which is, however, a low-key value-laden issue in the sense that the passion is not widespread in India but it does arise interesting ethical questions, some of which are basic to the recent ecological concerns. So let us have a look at the value-laden issue of practicing Bonsai (at a restricted level at our homes and at a wider level in horticultural departments) to have a glimpse of the real dynamics of applied ethics.

Before we delve into the real dynamics of ethical application, we should first of all take another task of justification, that is, the justification of Bonsai as a value-laden issue awaiting moral resolution. More than that, we have to justify that it is sensible to speak of the ethic of an Art as well as a Science called 'Bonsai'. Because Bonsai is called an "art" as well as a "science", and we need to argue first that there is something sensible in discussing the ethic of an art and a science. This is particularly useful because without an initial knowledge of the value-laden issue in consideration, nothing proceeds. We may not be able to frame a questionnaire for moral debate in the lack of such knowledge.

To call 'Bonsai' an 'art' is too trite, it needs clarification. Clarification is needed because we do not clearly understand the meaning of 'art' when it is used with 'Bonsai'. In fact, the term 'art' itself demands careful analysis for its meaning. Moreover, if any discussion about Bonsai has a philosophical relevance, it should be understood as the one falling in he field of Philosophy of Art, which may be subsumed under the broad field of Aesthetics, and one has to clarify what 'art' means to explain what 'philosophical study of art' means.

Philosophers generally believe after the later Wittgenstenian revolution that it is too odd to search for strict definitions of several terms or notions to clarify the meaning of those terms or notions. In fact, there may be no satisfactory definition at all. For instance, it may be enigmatic to strictly define 'philosophy' or 'ethics' or 'aesthetics' or 'art'. Nevertheless, we may define fine arts like "music", "painting" and so on but not "art" because an attempt to define 'art' may amount to either (a) laying down conditions (positive and negative) for distinguishing or evaluating a good from a bad art or (b) fall back on referring to an art and tell what it is and what it does or (c) do both (a) and (b). In case of (a) it is hardly any definition in the strict sense of the term (clarification of meaning through clear pronouncement of connotation and denotation of the terms) rather, it is a value-laden judgement about 'art' (good or bad). If we stick to (b) it is no definition of 'art' but statement of what some arts are and what are done in those arts. Whereas, if we go for (c), the position is no better; we do not define at all. Interestingly, many definitions, of 'art' have been given and they are at best definitions of convenience, that is, expression of what one thinks 'art' is. These definitions are either descriptive in nature or normative (what art should be like) and, therefore, fail to clarify the meaning of the term according to the several uses it may have. The situation is the same if we try desperately to descriptively define 'art' in terms of 'work of art'. It may be equally needless to tell what we do when we are involved with an art. Hence, attempts at defining 'art' may be a hopeless misadventure.

Nevertheless, we may on the one hand efficiently analyze the meaning of the term 'art' in different contexts and on the other hand analyze the meaning of the term 'art' in 'Philosophy of Art'. The latter task is broadly speaking a linguistic task, extremely important and basic to Philosophy, whereas the former is also a linguistic task, which is the core of Philosophy. Nevertheless, there is a difference in approach. If we go for the former linguistic inquiry, we have to take care of a great range of subjects and contexts wherein the notion 'art' has been used, conveying different meanings. If we allow this, it may be a huge encyclopedic effort in language use and meaning and we may be so enriched by a rainbow of meaning of 'art' that it may turn out to be a real hodge-podge. Nevertheless, it may be interesting enough and a sincere philosophical venture. Whereas, if we go for the 'analysis of the meaning' of 'art' in the expression, 'Philosophy of Art' and in the expression, 'the art of Bonsai', we may be restricting ourselves to a linguistic analysis, which although relatively narrow, turns out to be pragmatic in performing a definite philosophical task with which we are presently engaged. We should first start with an analysis of the meaning of 'art' in 'Philosophy of art'.

'Art' in 'Philosophy of art' first tells us about a philosophically relevant inquiry about all those human mental and/or physical efforts which, as opposed to the working of nature, are essentially 'artificial or man-made' so to say. One wonders about a philosophically relevant inquiry about manufactured artificialities. What could be the philosophically relevant way of inquiring about a manufactured pant for instance? The sense is not clear until we restrict ourselves to the range of objects (man-made) which demand care for an aesthetic evaluation or which demands care for the specific narrower function. Very broadly speaking, even a pant and a machine may demand care for aesthetic evaluation for they may affect our senses and mind in a unique manner (perhaps positively), in so far as their looks are pleasing, they are beautiful, they serve a purpose, they are symmetric and so on. But unfortunately we do not care too much for pants in philosophy or to be precise, in one of its branches, viz. Aesthetics. However, we do care for 'fine arts', which are as artificial as pants but which have been intentionally created for us not to be merely used (as pants) but to be viewed, read, heard, appreciated aesthetically. For instance, paintings, music, sculptures and Bonsai (we shall come to it later on). Thus, 'art' in 'philosophy of art' conveys the sense of those human creations, which are evaluated for not what they are intended to do rather, how they actually function in our experience. Yet, we may speak of many 'useful arts' which may not be so important a matter for philosophical inquiry. Even if we show some interest, it may be treated as secondary to 'fine arts' demanding attention for proper philosophical inquiry. It does not prevent us from aesthetically appraising a pant; it is nevertheless not needed in philosophical inquiry. More interesting may be aesthetic appreciation of an art, which is both fine and useful because it erases the primary and the secondary concerns in philosophical inquiry regarding art and tells us that 'art' in 'philosophy or art' means a deliberate human creation intended not merely to do something or serve a purpose but to do something and call for an aesthetic appreciation. In this sense, we may speak of 'architecture' as an 'art' and perhaps 'Bonsai' as an 'art'. In any case when I say that 'art' means such and such in 'philosophy of art', I am not giving any definition of 'art' or 'philosophy of art', I am analyzing the meaning of 'art' in 'philosophy of art'. Let us continue with this analysis.

The moment we speak of 'art' as a purposeful/useful as well as aesthetic human creation, we are reminded about the subject matter of an art. We may speak of subject matter of fine arts like painting and music (more popularly, 'theme'). Can we speak of a subject matter of Bonsai? Any way, 'art' is a creation bearing a theme or a subject matter. Moreover, 'art' in 'philosophy of art' conveys the sense that it may be treated as an image creation of object or objects in the world. In this sense, painting is an art, arguably music may be an art in this sense, literature is more doubtfully so. What about 'Bonsai'? Further, when we speak of 'art', we may mean a creation having a more or less non-conventional meaning. Literature is certainly an 'art' bearing a meaning for we may speak of direct references in this context but in other cases, 'meaning' is not so conventional. In such cases 'art' stands out as a creation having a meaningfully clear subject matter, which has a definite theme and a core focus or a thesis. If we keep these things in mind, we may speak of an art of music and painting, but can we speak of 'Bonsai' as an art in this sense? Still further, 'art' in 'philosophy of art' may mean a valuable act of human creation. The values being either sensuous or formal or life values.

Sensuous values consist in delight caused by the very phenomenal presentation of creation. Whereas formal values consist in the organization of the presented creation. It may be either structural of textural or it may be simply presented to us as an 'organic unity'. Whereas, apart from these mediumistic values, we may speak of life-values of an art that is the associative power of a creation that binds an art evaluator to life outside the medium of art. Certainly, painting is an art in this sense. We should try to see whether or not Bonsai is an art in these senses as well.

Hence, the moot issue is what is an art of Bonsai? Moreover, in what sense do we speak about this 'art' in philosophy of art? Another relevant question is, in what sense is Bonsai a science as well as an art? (It may be less debated that it is a science, but we have to consider this point as well). Further, we have to speak about the rationality of an ethic of science and art, and Bonsai as a science and an art. We shall consider these problems now.

'Science' is no less confusing than 'art' when in popular usage it is used as a discipline dealing with the objective study of the nature, natural objects and natural phenomena aided by observation and experiment. In fact, there will be hardly a normative science in this sense. Moreover, the term 'scientific' will lose its broad significance, viz. 'a systematic and methodical study'. If we keep this broad option open, only then can we speak of logic, ethics and aesthetics as normative science, which, however, do not take interest in 'what is' rather, considers 'what should be' as the most important one. Now, aesthetics being the broad field subsuming the philosophy of art, it would be appropriate to speak of a 'normative science of art' and philosophical reflection and criticism of issues arising out of this science is 'philosophy of art'. It may be a little difficult to justify a normative science of art because that does not fit into our way of thinking about science but it may not be difficult at all to justify that Bonsai is a science, lest we know what Bonsai consists in.

Bonsai is an artificial manipulation with plants and trees within a miniature scale and at a small space not by mechanically following the methods of horticultural science but rather through the application of aesthetic principles, metaphysical principles and common sense all at a time. Nevertheless, that it deals with plants and trees is indubitable. It may be thus categorized under the science of horticulture, which lays down principles for systematic and methodical manipulation with plants and trees for definite results. It is thus an objective science, bearing attributes of a positive science to a great extent in so far as it not merely lay rules of gardening (to be precise and simple), it applies those principles effectively in real objective situations (with plants and trees) involving a great degree of experimentation and careful observation. Not only this, horticulture cannot overlook the basic nature, structure and morphology of plants and trees for effective gardening. Thus, it is a scientific study in plants and trees as well. Nevertheless, horticulture being interested in laying down norms or principles for effective gardening and aesthetically appreciative gardening, it is also an art. It is thus a normative science as well. Bonsai being a specific mode of horticultural practice or a special application of gardening principles within a miniature scale and at a small space, it surely bears sign of sciences, positive and normative (as is with horticulture, the principal science). Thus, Bonsai would lay down effective principles of miniature gardening, apply those principles and study those plants and trees for their nature, structure and morphology. It would also like to freely observe and experiment on different patterns or styles of miniature gardening. Thus, Bonsai as a science follows basic horticultural techniques, essentially those used in ordinary gardening. Where Bonsai differs from ordinary gardening is in the aesthetic principles that it has to follow, that is, the norms it lays down for not mere miniature gardening but aesthetically appreciative miniature gardening. If this be so, we may speak of a normative science of art called 'Bonsai', as well as a positive science of miniature gardening called 'Bonsai'. Thus, Bonsai is a science by any extension of the term and indubitably an art.

Let us now consider the questions rose during discussion of nature of art and its meaning in the context of philosophy of art. In so far as 'art' in 'philosophy of art' conveys the sense of aesthetic human creations, which may be useful as well, Bonsai is certainly an 'art' in so far as it is such an artificial miniature creation of plants and trees by man, which demands a close aesthetic evaluation. Whether or not it is useful, although secondary, is nevertheless a crucial point, which we shall consider at a proper place. If we allow the usage 'the art of Bonsai' in this sense, it is not simply an artificiality, it is pleasing, beautiful, having a concern for pattern, a symmetry and for these reasons, Bonsai is an art in the aesthetic sense of the term. As far as it raises philosophically relevant question for further criticism, it should be discussed within philosophy of art. About whether or not Bonsai, like fine arts (*vis-à-vis* a more useful art), has a theme or a subject matter, are images of object or objects in the world, bears a meaning or a thesis and have values (sensuous or formal or life values), we may say that it does have a subject matter, a meaning and value which all fine arts have. Popular critics jokingly say that the only theme of Bonsai is to torture and make a plant disgraceful. In fact, the miniaturization has this negative effect on people's mind. Really speaking, every work of Bonsai has simple, common theme, 'complete transformation of an ordinary tree or plant into a spectacular work of art evoking aesthetic feelings in the creator and the onlooker'. Unlike many fine art forms, Bonsai is thus an utterly simple fine art having many styles but a common theme; this makes it an appeal-in-itself for the aesthetic evaluators striving for different styles. Stylistic differences need not end up in forming different schools of Bonsai as school of painting. However, stylistic difference may be looked upon a different mode of the aesthetic feelings creators may possess. About whether or not Bonsai is an image-art-creation the straightforward answer should be 'yes'. To quote master Bonsaist Peter Chan, "The miniature tree is only the artist's perception of reality—a picture or vision of the tree. The creative process is sparked off by the inspirational element, the medium of expression is the living plant and the final product is the image of reality".[1] Clearly, the complete transformation of a 'real tree' (it is not that Bonsai is unreal tree) into an 'image' is to say that artist's perception of a freely growing tree in nature is put in his garden, in a small space, in a beautiful new form—the miniature form (like an image of the real). This is to say that the so-called image reminds us of the 'real tree' or the freely growing tree in nature. If this were the case then Bonsai is no doubt imitation of the naturally growing trees. Neither will it be not proper to call them illusions in any sense of the term because a Bonsai artist does not attempt at evoking an aesthetic sense through creating illusions as do painters (at times) and magicians (quite often). A Bonsai artist tries to achieve something else through such aesthetic transformation of tree but for that, one has to look back to the Japanese-Chinese spiritual philosophy and the religious way of life. Even if a Bonsai artist do not know all this (I have a direct experience of many Bonsai experts who do not know anything about Taoism and Zen and the Wabi and the Sabi), his artistic image creation is chiefly aroused by a sense of fulfilment through image creation. This is essentially artistic in spirit, and therefore, Bonsai is an art. From this, it is very clear that Bonsai creation does have a focus or a clear thesis but it is often hidden to those who do not care for the 'metaphysic' of Bonsai.

The metaphysic of Bonsai is laid down in Taoism and Zen in terms of their distinctive philosophy of art or the metaphysic of art according to which, like every artistic venture, the technicalities, although vital, are secondary to the more primary goal of creating a beautiful art form in an uncontrived or in an essentially accidental manner. Thus an artist is the one who is not hankering for creation in a completely artificial manner, rather, the artist becomes an effective source for chance happenings so that the sense of "I-ness" in creation vanishes. The creator-creation relation is not external, the creator is the vital source of an internal aesthetic urge to create and when this urge is expressed in an uncontrived way, the real creation is before us. Thus the core or thesis of the art of Bonsai is. "to become a source of chance-creation (in this case miniature creation of trees)". One, who understands this, would understand the humility that is needed for a Bonsai creation. The ultimate expression of this humility could be seen in using this art form not as a drawing room decoration item, rather placing a work or art in the "tokonoma" (in Japanese culture) as an act of worship. The thesis of Bonsai is thus fitting to his act having a deep spiritual significance. The notion of "art" in the Tao and the Zen fits with the Bonsai creation; it is thus an "art" in this sense. It would be expecting too much from the global citizens interested in Bonsai that they should have a spiritual feeling or they should understand the metaphysic of Bonsai, and, therefore, it is not a necessary precondition of Bonsai to know its metaphysic. Indians, for instance, even those who are deeply involved in Bonsai, do not adorn their worship places with Bonsai plants but they have the practice of putting handmade garlands in worship places and around the deities, they worship. Nevertheless, this does not prevent them from being true Bonsai lovers and practitioners unless they lack basic humility and sense of aesthetic principles in Bonsai practice. A sense of decorating and showing of the luxury may be devoid of such humility no doubt.

Bonsai is an art in the sense of having sensuous, formal and life values. It has a definite sensuous value because it is able to evoke aesthetic feelings in man, however its aesthetic appreciation vary from the one who is influenced by a work of Bonsai art. Its formal value lies in the different organized presentation of the work of art and beyond the corporeal to the metaphysical or the spiritual. Moreover, it may be said to have a life-value in a more pragmatic sense, that is, Bonsai works may be restored, cared and nourished in horticulture departments and elsewhere in societies (even in households at a limited scale) for the preservation of different species of plants and trees, particularly those having great botanical value and those rapidly vanishing on earth. This is the usefulness of the art or the pragmatics of Bonsai as an art. Thus, Bonsai as a normative science of art is altogether a useful art as well.

With this we come to conclude that in the expression 'the art of Bonsai', "art" should be taken as a 'fine art' as well as 'useful art' concerned with the miniaturization of plants and trees through systematic and scientific techniques (horticultural) and following basic aesthetic principles. The objects of such an art should be artistic fulfilment and it should be pragmatic (socially, culturally, religiously and scientifically).

It is clear that a proper understanding and evaluation of the ethic of the art called "Bonsai" is possible in the Indian context only if we are aware of the philosophical-religious background of this art, which grew and flourished in the Japanese Zen tradition in particular and in China. Moreover, we have to know the basics of the garden aesthetics of the Japanese tradition *vis-à-vis* the Western traditions and the place of the work of Bonsai in such gardening traditions. We may take a few cues from this to make a contrast and comparison with the Indian gardening tradition and the place of the role of Bonsai in it. This is needed in so far as to provide us with the most important arguments in favour of the ethicality of this art form. If we are aware of these strong ethical arguments in favour of Bonsai (which stems from its perennial place of practice), we may further evaluate them in the face of the antagonists' counter arguments of unethicality of Bonsai.

In the Japanese tradition, the arts of Bonsai and Ikebana are not taken as mere decorative value. Because we have to know about the inherent spirit of the Zen, first to evaluate these art forms. Avoiding all details of the Zen, we may simply state that according to the Zen the ultimate essence of man is not in the paradise but in our heart, which has to be revealed from within. This revelation within leads us to a unique mystery experience, the Satori experience of ultimate truth. This is a state of consciousness in which the duality of the world has ceased to exist. It is only through deep contemplation or *dhyāna* that the "*prajñā*" latent in every mind could be known. This spirit of Zen, spirit of realizing the ultimate through deep contemplation is possible if we are simple and tranquil. The tea ceremony or the cha-no-yu is one instance of such serenity and tranquillity. Bonsai and Ikebana are other instances. Nevertheless, the difference is that in the cha-no-yu we are right at the contemplative mood, whereas in the latter we are portraying our realization of the truth more or less indirectly through a work of art. The latter may be thus one way to show that the truth has been revealed to us and the art forms are expressions of this revelation. It is perhaps due to this that Bonsai (also Ikebana) is not merely an art form but an art form conveying a deeper truth inherent in artist's consciousness. It is, therefore, pure and unblemished, Hence, all Bonsai works express the natural simplicity and serenity or what is Wabi and that it is inostentious and tranquil or what is Sabi. So every work of Bonsai need to be guided by the basic principles of the Wabi and the Sabi because this is prerequisite of our expression of deep metaphysical realization. Bonsai is thus ethically desirable in so far as it is an expression of the inner realization of the truth in a most serene and inostentious manner. This work of beauty is not for pleasing eyes for conveying realized person's experience. It is perhaps due to this that Bonsai works have been traditionally placed in the worship places or in tokonoma in Japanese household. The Japanese cultural fabric may be thus expressed as pure aesthetics or bee-gha-ku. However during my visit to this country some Bonsai practitioners told me that in modern Japan one may not find tokonoma in households, what to speak of Bonsai works to adore worship places. Unsurprisingly, both to have a tokonoma and to place Bonsai pots just for household decoration have creeped in the modern Japanese culture. It is equally true for China, particularly after the official philosophy have dominated the "Chan" (meditative Buddhism) and its aesthetic associates like the works of Bonsai. Then the question of the moral desirability of Bonsai just on the basis of traditional religion and mysticism is at stake. The ethic of an art called "Bonsai" has to be differently grounded.

Although Bonsai itself is not gardening practice, it can easily be a part of that practice. Here it is interesting to notice that among many gardening practices, pruning of hedge boundaries and pruned decorative trees are very common and popular. Many people draw a parallel to say that the pruning of the hedges is what Bonsai like practice in the garden is. Many continue to say that if we can prune hedges to look more disciplined in growth, look symmetric, beautiful and useful (as a boundary) and all this is ethically permissible, what is wrong with disciplining the growth of a black pine for instance? In doing so, the pine looks symmetric, beautiful and useful (for it is restoration of a rare species). Nevertheless, the parallel is not so good because pruning the hedges is a gardening practice having different rules for nurturing and growth whereas Bonsai practice at a small place and at a small space is not strictly following such nurturing and growth rules. It is in fact a practice of art with trees and plants, which nevertheless, may be placed in pots in small or big gardens as a part of the beautification of gardens alongside other miniature gardening works. I have seen many gardens (private and public) in India in which, Bonsai works have been placed at strategic points for an aesthetically beautiful look to the garden. This could be seen in modern Japanese garden. The one in the Centre for International Studies in Tokyo had one such tiny garden with some miniature works on trees alongside other works. Nevertheless, in such gardens we may find some pruned trees and plants rooted to the soil and not in the trays in artificial manipulated forms. Those pruned trees and plants attached to the perennial soil, is a different miniature gardening practice and need not be confused with Bonsai works. Hence, the argument, "hedges are to Bonsai" will not work. What we get is that any pruning and dwarfing practice in gardens is not Bonsai work and, therefore, the justification of one cannot be extended in the case of the other. I remember that a staunch Bonsaist once asked me, why Indians pluck flowers from flowering plants to make garlands if Bonsai was so unethical for its typical pruning practices? I wonder how this parallel could work. Because plucking flowers to make a garland (beautiful ones of course) is not like Bonsai work, which is a manipulation with live tree. Not so all practices of plucking, shedding leaves or petals, cutting etc. need be necessarily treated as Bonsai works.

Yet, even if Bonsai has been shifted from its basic Zen tradition and placed to the modern gardens as a part of gardening beautification (not practice), some basic principles of gardening practice need to be followed even in case of Bonsai. So to think that Bonsai has nothing to do with common scientific gardening practices, would be wrong. Among basic gardening practices like watering, loosening the soil, adding essential nutrients for plant survival, cutting unnecessary growths, plucking yellowing leaves etc. are important for Bonsai works as well. What is different is that Bonsai follows other rules of dwarfing and beautifying a plant, which is not needed in common gardening practices. Nevertheless, both common gardening practices and Bonsai within the Zen tradition follow common basic spiritual rules as well. If we do not understand this, we will never understand and evaluate the gardening practices in Japan as a whole and we will never know why in such gardens, Bonsais make a special significance. Langdon Warner thinks that the fundamental thing about Japanese gardens and what sets them apart from any garden of the civilized world is usually lost sight by westerners. It is the fact that the art was definitely used in China and Japan to express the highest truth of religion and philosophy. Something of the spiritual symbolism has been expressed in the garden laid out by the Zen philosophers."

When we speak of garden, says Shin-ichi Anzai in his essay, "Is the world a Garden?' We have to keep in mind the fact that a garden is literally a real part of the earth's surface. One has this feeling when one looks at a garden from the top, flying in an aeroplane. The feeling is conjoined with another one, which is the sense of demarcation or a boundary. Although when we look from the top, we also have a feeling of vanishing boundaries as well because the gardens give way to wilderness and the wilderness to the stratosphere making the space the frontier and the earth one garden. Nevertheless, when we are on earth, and the garden is rooted to the earth, gardens are enclosed entities denying universality. This is the main reason why the gardens in the west has been conceived as entities marginalized both spatially and temporally. On the other hand, we have the Japanese-Chinese gardens, which although as naturalistic as the western garden, nevertheless they are emphatically open and serenely natural'.

Hence, in the Chan and the Zen traditions explains Anzai, the garden grows out emphatically open and natural but are giving way to artificiality and conventionality in the pressure of the marginalized Western garden techniques. Nevertheless, artificiality and conventionality are compatible with the serenity and naturalness. There is thus no distinction between the art, the beautification and naturalness in the Chinese and Japanese gardening traditions. So even if we have in the modern times shifted from the tokonoma to the petty gardens within a concrete stylized building framework, the art and the naturalness with simplicity could be still realized in these gardens. This is perhaps the oldest taboo that rules in the subconscious psyche of the gardeners of these traditions. The gardener is thus supposed to emancipate from a narrow individualistic self to embrace a bigger nature. A Zen priest and gardener Muso Soseki says, "those who believe that mountains, rivers, earth, grass, trees, stones and pebbles are nothing but their own nature will soon make the seasonal variables of the natural world just the occasions for their enlightenments. If one makes various arts too ostentatious a means of self-assertion, they will turn out to be only evil".[2] The garden is thus according to the Zen, for praying, to serve something that bigger than the self is. This is clearer if we happen to go to the cha-no-yu garden, where even a trash bin, fountains, thatched huts and toilets (the utilities) merge with artistic, the serene and the humble.

Now take the art of Bonsai, even though globalization has shifted the Bonsai to a more naturalistic, artistic garden where the Japanese garden is clearly under the threat of the western beautification, the pots of Bonsai works placed imaginatively alongside those trees and plants fixed to their perennial places (big or small) would create a sense of serenity, inostention, humbleness and open-naturalness. This is at least what the modern adherents of the Bonsai would imagine. Hence, the conceivable arguments in favour of the ethical desirability that stems out of religious-philosophical zeal of the Zen would now give way to the more deep rooted humane elements of the creator of the piece of art. The adherents would now leave the prayer and the dedication to the higher self to stick to the elements of simplicity, humbleness or the basics of the Wabi and the Sabi. Any way, Bonsai would have either in its favour a religious argument, or humane arguments, both are not so disjoint and this justify that the art is ethical no doubt.

Interestingly, outside the Chinese-Japanese garden tradition, for instance, in India, where the naturalist gardens of the towns and cities are clearly under the pressure of the Western demarcation and artificiality in beautification (even in the household gardens), the placing of Bonsai works may lack this basic spirit of Zen or even the humane elements in the artists. It is doubtful whether or not most of the Bonsai practitioners are aware of what are the guiding norms of Bonsai, i.e., what is there in the Wabi and the Sabi. No one can really demand that the artist should be a follower of Zen. Then there must be different argument here from the protagonists and from the antagonists. However, we have to keep in mind the basic arguments of the protagonists, which have already been stated. How can we know all this if we are not talking to people? How do we get an idea of the moral opinion of the people about Bonsai if we do not talk to the antagonists and the protagonists (preferably bringing them to a debate)? How is it possible to analyze the moral arguments of these people to know about which ethical theory or theories have been dynamic or have been applied in the cases of value-laden problems like this one? Clearly, we have to go for an intersubjective corroboration dialogue. Let us come to it now.

After I was awarded the Major Research Project Work "Applied Ethics in Indian Context" by the University Grants Commission with effect from January 1997, I decided to undertake the resolution of the some value-laden ecological/environmental issues to start with (the methodology of resolution being intersubjective corroboration). On the 20th day of March 1998, I arranged the first "Intersubjective corroboration dialogue" in my department and the value-laden issue was "Why Bonsai"? I think the readers remember what this methodology consists of. As per the scheme, I have to justify first why Bonsai should be considered a value-laden issue needing ethical resolution. In fact, it all started with an article in a popular Bengali bi-monthly magazine, which published reactions of those who thought Bonsai to be unethical or what they called the darker side of Bonsai practice. The debate attracted me not for the lively style of the articles but for the ethical orientation and the moral arguments of the antagonists followed by those of the protagonists. In the mean time, I had a chance to visit a cactus-cum-Bonsai exhibition in greater Calcutta. For three consecutive days of the exhibition, I was going to the exhibition to get a first hand feeling of what people felt about the Bonsai work and to realize myself what I felt. Then I started searching some people in Ranchi who had this passion of Bonsai to find out what they felt. This was particularly useful for me because inter-subjective corroboration being essentially dependant on fair samples of ethical opinions, it had to start from my place of work and then spread to other parts of the country (which was a difficult task for it needed a lot of financial and human resource). Any way it has to be started with whatever paltry amount was sanctioned to me.

It was interesting to talk to the Bonsaists in Ranchi. First, I was unaware of the fact that they have a large association, which met annually in an exhibition in the Agricultural College premises in Ranchi in the annual "Krishi Mela" (Agricultural Fair). Second, they were all aware of the ethical questions and were keen at participating in an ethical debate. So first, I got the idea that as the antagonists had a lot to speak about, so had the protagonists. Indubitably, Bonsai was value-laden issue to be considered for moral resolution for both parties were aware of ethical questions (although none was ethics-trained).

Bonsai raises many metaphysical and religious questions but to me, the concern now is that it raises ethical questions, which, we like or not, we have to face. Perhaps we cannot avoid many ethical questions pertaining to different arts. One reason for this is that an intentional human act, which affects other sentient and non-sentient beings, raises question of oughtness and rightness. Why should we do such and such things? Is the key to such questions? Interestingly, a simplistic way is to challenge the validity of such questions but it may be sophistical and not rational. It is better if we face them. Hence, we should understand that in "the ethic of Bonsai," "ethic" signifies those problems or issues raised in moral discourse or those pertaining to ethics, viz., those of "rightness" and "oughtness" or more precisely, "desirableness". If we address to these questions, we would justify (morally) that Bonsai, as an art is not merely desired and done, it is rather, desirable and valuable (this distinction is crucial in an ethical discussion). The justification of the moral value of doing Bonsai would thus erase all negative doubts about it (like the most popularly heard, “they dwarf it”, “they immorally prune it” etc.) Thus, an inquiry about ethical validity of the art of Bonsai is a philosophical inquiry, and if we justify the validity, we may justify the ‘ethic’ of Bonsai or the moral basis of Bonsai. In other words, Bonsai-talk involves ethics-talk.

The readers, however, should be told about why practice of Bonsai was classified under the “value-laden ecological/ environmental issue”. The immediate reason was that Bonsai is an art form dealing with the dwarfing of live plants and trees through unique mechanical techniques, along-with specific gardening techniques. The dwarfing was done at very small space. Sometimes the whole work could be easily removed from the tray with a feeling that paltry nutrition was supplied for that was enough for the dwarfed tree or plant. Now such dwarfing particularly attracts us when we look at other dwarfed plant and trees fixed to their perennial places, and, therefore, does not lack in nutrition, and when we look at freely growing trees and plants particularly those, which have been dwarfed in a Bonsai work. In the first case of dwarfed plants, the techniques applied were only mechanical (like pruning) whereas in the second case, there was least human intervention. However, we do find some natural deficiencies or natural interventions when a tree becomes dwarfed but that is not Bonsai, for it is essentially a human intervention mechanically as well as scientifically. Now these factors taken together, gives us a feeling that man must have started intervening knowingly or intentionally for whatever reasons with live trees and plants in the present alarming situation of dwindling green forests, fading natural wilderness, decrease in the foliage area, decrease in photosynthetic activity, imbalance in the basic life cycle and energy cycle causing greenhouse effect, global famines, floods and so on. We are also attracted towards the fact that given this alarming ecological crises owing to so many factors (and not owing to Bonsai practice), why not save more and more dwindling species of plants and trees in artistic and pragmatic way like Bonsai? So negatively or positively an idea creeps in our mind that Bonsai is some such practice which has to do something with the present ecological crises. Does it have a more alarming effect on ecology or does it help us in averting it? With this, we come to see that the moral questions regarding Bonsai are in fact deeper and trifling ecological questions. Therefore, we are at hand questions involving many things—ethicality (desirability of Bonsai practice so to say), ecological concern and artistic concern. What is interesting is to notice that the ecological and the artistic concerns are interwoven with the ethical concern.

The next task for me was to prepare a panel for the moral discussion. There was a need to prepare a questionnaire and to supply it to the participants to enable themselves to prepare for the debate.

First two to three questions were framed so as to gauge the general ethical outlook of the participants and then to move on to more and more controversial questions having sharp ethical orientation to end up with practical questions regarding decision making after the participants have reached a consensus.

The participants were mainly botanists, horticulturists, philosophers, artists and people having different professions. The Bonsaists, teachers, students and common people attending the discourse had a chance to make important inquiries and to express their opinions. The entire discourse was conducted by me and was recorded. The selection of the participants needed care because we have to keep in mind the balance of the antagonists and the protagonists as well as to search for those people who are not only amateur Bonsaists but in favour of the ethicality of Bonsai. This is possible only if we are very careful about talking to people while fixing up our expert's panel. We should be careful as ethicists whenever we talk to the people requesting to participate in a debate. We have to be precise and simple and let people know easily why their participation is ethically important. We may have initial problems in making people understand what "ethics" really is. Soon they know what we are speaking about. Interestingly this is true for even those people (whom I invited for other debates) having little or no formal education. Nevertheless, we should be careful about framing questions. Sometimes, we need purely simple question, sometimes a little grave ones and yet again, some enriched ones. The questions should be put in a language easily understood by the participants. Here, however, the questionnaire will be presented in English for the benefit of the English readers. The most important thing is that even if we are pressed too hard, do not indulge in any debate with a person we have gone to select because that will disclose our favour or disfavour as ethicist and the participant may either take our side thinking that philosophers would like this line and then conceal what he or she really thinks or may refuse to take part in the debate thinking that he or she may cross swords with a lot of people and get cornered. We should also avoid putting ethical questions to the participants before we have selected them for the debate. Tell the participants not to go through any book of ethics. Tell them to be free from any prejudice about a moral theory. Tell them not to go to a philosopher guide. A golden rule is to avoid philosophers to participate in such debates along with other non-philosophers. Philosophers act best as audience when they raise interesting questions or protests or even correct other views and add something to what has been said. This naturally forms a part of the dialogue later on. The golden rule is to be followed because philosophers are co-opted people and have a tendency for moral engineering. However, when they face a range of ethical views in a dialogue, they may act as good critics and often come out with their views in a more open fashion. However, this is possible only if we have the dialogue at a place where some philosophers are present. At times after a debate, we feel the need to talk to many other people, including the philosophers regarding the point already corroborated and decision taken. Only then, we feel further need of interviewing people and collection of responses through written replies. For collecting written responses, we have to inform about the main questions, points of corroboration and decision taken. In fact, in country like India, several such discourses at several places should be conducted. Moreover, this is a team effort, which I tragically did not have. Given the academic growth of practical ethics in India, and the philosophers' theoretical jugglery in this field, we are already in the trap of ethical engineering. There is really no application of ethics in applied ethics in India if we do not go in the way of talking to people for moral resolution. Hence, people's ethics should replace phoenix ethics. However, we shall come to it later on.

The participants in the corroboration dialogue were Dr. Ram Dayal Munda, the former Vice-Chancellor of Ranchi University, who was also the head of the department of Tribal Languages in the same university and specialist in aesthetics. This selection was for his deep study in aesthetics and because he champions the rights of the people of tribal land facing vast forest depletion. He is also vocal about the ecological crises in the tribal land particularly owing to the misadventure of the trouble shooters (*diku*) engaged in forest depletion. I have selected Dr. K.K. Nag, head of the department of Botany of Ranchi University for his open antagonism of Bonsai culture. Prof. Nag specializes in tissue culture. The selection of Dr. T.K. Ghosh was natural as he is another botanist of the same university and was open to oppose Bonsai practice. He specializes in plant taxonomy. The selection of Dr. N. Dayal, another botanist from Ranchi University was owing to his support for Bonsai practice. Although he specializes in plant genetics and ecological science, he is also an outspoken utilitarian having a M.Sc. degree in Marxist philosophy from Moscow University. Dr. B.P. Jain, the head of the department of Horticulture in the Birsa Agriculture University in Ranchi was selected for his protagonist view as well as for his technical knowledge of Bonsai. Not only this, he himself practices Bonsai at home and his department has a phenomenal Bonsai bank. Then I selected three other Bonsaists of Ranchi Bonsai Association, Dr. P. Dey, a pathologist by profession, Mr. A.K. Chatterjee, Development Officer in the Life Insurance Corporation in Ranchi, Mr. S.K. Sengupta, a retired officer of the Central Coalfield Ltd. and Mr. S. Chanda, officer in the Sriram Bearings Ltd. and a celebrated Bonsaists in India. I also selected Dr. R.S. Singh, the head of the Hindi department for his outspoken antagonism to Bonsai and for his knowledge of aesthetics. The head of my department, Dr. K.K.L. Karna, five other teachers and number of students, teachers of other colleges and departments participated in the discourse as honourable audience, who at the end made the whole debate extremely interesting by putting a number of questions, giving suggestions for corroboration and for decision-making rules.

Let us now come to the structure of the questionnaire. Normally an ethicist or other interested people have to prepare an elaborate questionnaire, carefully micro-analyze so that the participants may ponder over those questions to prepare their minds properly. This also helps them in understanding what really is going to happen in the debate. Then we have to prepare a precise questionnaire, some five to six well-farmed questions, which bring out the best of the moral opinions of the people. My experience is that if you move with five such questions with bubbling six to seven participants and the audience, you will cross three hours in a whisker. Therefore, we have to be careful about putting too many questions. This is to avoid boredom after some time. Objective questions does not fit here because ethical questions are best replied when they are put in a manner such that the participants feel a lot of subjective freedom in unfolding their views.

It is very important to know how to put these questions one by one after satisfactory responses have been gathered for each question. Disagreement or cross arguments should not be allowed to cross a limit. One interesting way to put these questions is to start with an antagonist first by quoting a short passage from a book or an article or a newspaper clipping which may incite the thought process of the participants in so far as the passage has been unequivocally pro-Bonsai for instance, and it gives us a feeling that the passage is noteworthy for it appears at an important place. It is essential to fix some time for each response before we move on to other responses. In the meantime it is important for an ethicist to aptly listen to the moral responses, note the moral hitches and the fallacies underlying each response, we should be very careful about cutting short some such responses midway when the replies goes astray, that is, surpasses the moral orientation to become more personal or too technical or too theoretical.

Given this background, let us now pass on to the questions and the debate. Here as we go on with the debate, our task is to state clearly the moral opinions first, then we shall identify the points of corroboration and finally, the decision making rules. We shall further undertake the important task of the ethicists, that is, the post-corroboration analysis of the moral opinions to find out the dynamics of the normative theories and weigh their relative strengths and weaknesses.

A common sense question to start the discourse, a question as I said, to gauge the basic moral standpoint of a participant is to ask, *What in your opinion should be the role of man in an ecological community?* Readers should notice that the question is the one pertaining to morality with a distinct use of "should" in it, meaning thereby not, what the participant thinks a man does within the ecological community rather, what is expected of him as a morally charged member to do. More clearly, there is a hidden sense of desirability in this question, i.e., to ask what is "desirable" for a member of an ecological community to do? What I found from the replies given to this basic question is that the participants were speaking about (a) the position of man in the ecological community, (b) the relation of man and other members of the ecological community, (c) the value of man—other relation in this community, and (d) most importantly, what is expected from us, that is how we should live in this community. This final response was often mixed with what ought to be the end (or summum bonum) of human life. However, not all participants were vocal about this. Yet all were conscious about the fact that in so far as human action towards the ecological community at large needs to be judged for their moral value or moral worth such and such are the criteria for such value or worth. Once you find clear response about the criteria of moral evaluation of the intentional actions of human beings, you find the participants' idea about end of human life. Often a not-so-careful participant may go on stretching his opinion to the extent that the basic position is antagonized by him and you are in hand a number of moral ideals and criteria of moral judgement. Another truism is that never expect too much from the non-philosophers. For instance, do not imagine that what one's opinion is in the context of Bonsai about moral criteria or moral ideal should be as uniform as well in the case of euthanasia. Because the moral opinion of these people in any way is not academically fine-tuned, well thought out and weighted for justification. Nevertheless, this is not a drawback. We have to remember that in applying ethics, participants are applying their common ethical knowledge and not that they are deliberately applying one academic theory or the other. Yet, when they apply their moral knowledge in a real case like Bonsai, they are very sincere and very open. If ethicists have the ability to ponder over ethical matters during post-corroboration analysis, a likelihood of a reflection of an academic moral theory is very high. Any ethicist involved in the dynamics of application of ethics in moral resolution in the society need to be careful about making hasty judgements regarding the moral ideal and moral criteria advocated by a person. One task of an ethicist is to remain alert during the whole discourse and whenever there is a chance to point out the remarkable shift in one's opinion about this basic matter so that the person falls in self-contradiction, it has to be immediately pointed out. In due course, the person either returns to his basic position to give up the present argument or wants to revise his basic position. In any case, he is shown to be at fault. Such people dwelling in doubts should be carefully dealt with, and if he wants to give up an argument in the face of sticking to his basic moral view, he should be given a chance for renewed argument. But one who changes his or her basic position too quickly, should be given another chance as well but then he has to stick to his new position and arguments following thereof or else we have to be calculative in putting further question to him or her. During analysis and closure, such views need not be seriously taken. Really, you cannot follow a policy of tolerance when it comes to resolution and decision-making because that has far-reaching social ramification. Let us remember that we cannot read beforehand the argumentative disposition of a participant, so we have to be a critic, a moderator and a corrector in ethical application.

Let us return to the responses to this basic question. Without entering into an explanation of every response, it may be mentioned that the participants advocated three views. First view is that "man being the most evolved species in the ecological community, is like a spider in a cobweb and his actions in this closely knit community should be the sustenance of the ecological community despite optimum use of it for the general welfare of the human race". Second position is that "man being insuperably liked to the entire ecological community, his desirable actions ought to be such that it leads to the realization of the truth that all beings high and low, animate and inanimate are essentially divine. Hence human actors should be evaluated in view of not following the rule of the divine but to realize the divine in ecological community". Third, some participants were of opinion that "man being the crown of evolution, his action should be such that an unthreatened existence of one's self has been guaranteed first. Only then do we think of others otherwise there will be none to think of great ecological ideals here. The first reply, simply stated, is welfaristic (not utilitarian in its vogue). The second is unhesitatingly a pantheistic ethical doctrine. It need not be confused with monotheistic ethical ideal any way (at least in this case) because there is no reference to the "realization of the one Supreme Reality" or something like that. However, this does remind us of the fact that everything being "divine", there must be at least one Being who by virtue of his Self has permeated the entire existence because he has either created or manifested everything in his own light. Then the Being is hopefully one and the Creator of all existence. However, some participants did not indulge in such metaphysical churnings. They simply stated that the entire ecological community is essentially not material but divine, so it has to be realized like that and the realization comes not by pure thought but through living a community life of purity, (that is respecting all forms of existence as divine). Anyway, this view is uniquely ideal, far more difficult to follow than the first one. The third, one was simple. It stated the simplest version of egoism. Mind it; it is not egotism for it has nothing to do with the pleasure satisfaction of one's own self.

Readers should be careful here to notice that in the mean time, what I have done is not a plain statement of the moral ideals or the moral standards of the participants, I have analyzed their views or responses to filter out such theories, which were basic to their further judgements about Bonsai. This task undertaken by me is what is post-corroboration task of ethicist, which may be special to them; other parties interested in it therefore need another thing—an academic training in wholesome ethics. So academic ethics does have something in store for ethicists but it has little to do with the real life application of ethical knowledge, for the best ethicists may fall prey to ethical engineering and ethical bossing if his academics are taken too far. Ethical application is essentially intersubjective corroboration backed up by the analyses of the moral debate.

Now we have to identify 'who is who', that is, we have to classify the antagonists and the protagonists according to the responses obtained above. Interesting is to notice that among the antagonists as well as the protagonists, there were differences with regard to the basic moral opinion. Take the antagonists for instance, Dr. R.S. Singh, and most of the teachers of philosophy who advocated the 'pantheistic ethical ideal' *vis-à-vis* botanists like Dr. K.K. Nag and Dr. T.K. Ghosh who advocated 'welfarism'. However, when we turn to the protagonists we find that the house is a peculiar association both 'egoism' and 'welfarism' because almost all of them, the professional botanist and the horticulturist (Dr. Dayal and Dr. Jain) and the entire group of Bonsaists were maintaining the position that although man is the most important being in the ecological community and there is nothing ethical in neglecting the primacy of his own well-being, the well-being of the entire human race along with the sustenance of the other members of the ecological community is important as well. In fact what they advocated is that the general well-being of the ecological community including that of the human beings is not at all antagonized to the well-being of the individual human beings because there is no point in speaking about the 'general welfare' where 'individual welfare' has been overlooked, yet, when we speak of the relative importance of the two, botanist and the horticulturist appeared to be more in favour of welfarism than egoism whereas Bonsaists were primarily egoists than welfarists. There is thus no doubt that welfarists are egoists (and not upholders of pure-benevolence) in some sense but there is a transition from "I" to "We" in their moral opinion. This has to be understood clearly. Hence, they would not be treated as antagonistic to the basic proposition of the Bonsaists. What is most interesting is that the Bonsaists were conscious about showing no strong liking towards the pantheistic view, whereas the antagonists had no serious objection to the welfarism stated by some of the protagonists. The Bonsaists, however, were not completely agreeing that pantheism goes against Bonsai practice and the antagonists were not completely agreeing that welfarism goes in favour of Bonsai practice. What is more interesting is to notice that welfarism as such cannot count as a theory either against or in favour of Bonsai practice. This is a good example to remember that a monolithic mind in application of ethics would soon discover the mistake that any one ethical theory cannot be artificially applied to decide the ethicality or unethicality of an intentional practical action. In the same way, perhaps pantheistic ethics may be taken as the basis of the morality as well as immorality of an intentional practical action. Nevertheless, this sounds strange. Why should it be like this? Is there an apparent fallacy inherent in the entire affair of ethical application? Alternatively, is the entire affair a damp squib?

No, there is nothing wrong in either the ethical theories or ethical application. In fact in real cases of ethical application (as in the case of Bonsai), the participants do not artificially apply ethical theory but they apply their common ethical knowledge, which may reflect the basics of an ethical theory about which we come to know in theoretical ethics. Hence, the participants being completely unaware of the established theories go on unfolding their ethical knowledge uninhibitedly, which, when analyzed at the post-corroboration stage reveals that even those who are theoretically untrained in ethics might advocate one ethical theory or the other, thereby breaking the myth that theories of ethics are intellectual generalizations by gifted people, passed on to us (the ethicists), which we can now use in fitting cases. The truth is that our common knowledge pertaining to ethical matters might reflect any of these theories about which we are completely unaware. Further, the basic non-cooption with academic ethics is the reason why there may be serious disagreement about the fruits of a theory, that is, about what are the implications of a theory. This is why welfarist ethical ideal may be used effectively by the Bonsaists to hold that the art is welfaristic whereas some argue that the art is against general welfare of the eco-community. Let us clarify this to some extent. The Bonsaists supporting welfarism thinks that general welfare being our ethical ideal, we should go for such gardening practices like Bonsai, which may enable us to restore the endangered plant species like black-pine because that will be a means to the general welfare. To add more to it, general welfare may include the flourishing of the artistic endeavour in the society. Hence if welfarism is the well-accepted ethical principle, the Bonsaists derive major ethical arguments, from what follows from the acceptance of it. Whereas when welfarism is used by the antagonists (botanists), the secondary rules, which they derive, may be completely different. They may hold that dwarfing techniques hinder the basic disposition of the freely flourishing tree, the tree that we desperately need in the face of depleting forest cover and diminishing foliage. Thus dwarfing is against the welfare of the plants and trees, and against everything depending on plants and trees. Moreover, restoration of endangered plant species may be done differently, that is, following other scientific techniques. Finally, artists' welfare does not merely depend on Bonsai practice; it may be rather against their welfare because dwarfing practice may boomerang on them as well when an ecological crisis is taken into account. Therefore, the secondary rule that follow may be quite different. What we find is that even the best brain in ethics (what to speak on non-ethicists) may differ regarding what follows from the basic ethical principle, that is, what secondary rules ought to be derived. Particularly, in case of resolution of value-laden cases this amount, to a real problem, the problem of fixing one ethical theory as the basis of ethical evaluation of all kinds. We may be careful to notice that neither ethical theory can be accepted as the only standard to judge all moral actions and decisions nor can one theory be taken as a tool to resolve all moral crises including the case of Bonsai. So rather than arguing about which argument from welfarism was valid (protagonists' or antagonists') we should better keep in mind how the proponents of different ethical theories as well as the proponents of different ethical arguments assemble to come to a moral consensus. What we got thus far is that any cooption with theories will not do in ethical resolution.

When we come to egoism (of the Bonsaists) and the pantheistic ethics (of the antagonists), we must remember that any theory need not be declared as the one, which rules supreme over the consensus. It is also not true to think that despite strong objections to pantheistic ethics by the atheists (protagonists Dr. Dayal and Dr. Jain), they were averse to moral corroboration. What we now discover is that no one theory, for instance, welfarism by itself or unilaterally and unopposed might resolve ethical impasse involved in Bonsai. Therefore, the case of ethical application is not one of artificial application of one or more standard ethical theories in value-laden cases. Thus, artificial way of applying ethics is not applying ethics at all, it is something more. It is a matter of scrutinizing what follows from a moral dialogue, and subsequently finding out how disagreements lead to agreement or to moral resolution and how decisions are taken. It is also interesting to analyze how different ethical theories emerge in moral dialogue, become active, cross swords, are interpreted, debated, criticized and are *transcended* to come to moral agreement. All this is within applied ethics. It is interesting here to notice that the normative theory which appeared to fall to a disgrace (much comforting to the anti-theorists), in fact has risen from the ashes (thanks to post-corroboration analysis). This is the true 'return to theories'.

Moving beyond the theory debate now, we may look at the next few questions, which are more related to Bonsai. One crucial question is about the freedom of the vegetable kingdom. I asked *do you conceive of a basic freedom to all vegetable life forms?* This question was enough to stimulate the other (which I did not ask) but was naturally raised by the participants themselves and debated at length. It was, *whether or not Bonsai went against the basic freedom of plants and trees*. In fact, this question was discussed to such an extent that the main issue, namely ethicality of Bonsai practice was naturally covered. If we turn to the welfarist botanists who are antagonists (Dr. Ghosh and Dr. Nag), we get three arguments drawn from their basic ethical position: (a) the argument from the balance in nature, (b) the argument from human likeness, and (c) the argument from anti-selfishness.

The first of three is a popular one supported by almost all antagonists and no protagonists challenged this argument. There are reasons for this. The argument draws strength from the basic scientific truth that the ecological community being a network of interdependent life forms as well as inanimate entities, all members of this community is of equal importance. However, these members, barring intellectually evolved man, are unable to raise voice for the basic right to live freely, that is, live without destruction and subjugation. It follows that this interdependent network of existence is a fine-tuned balanced existence. There is an energy balance in an inherent relation of interdependence. Now if we start Bonsai practice at a more and more wider scale, it goes against the freedom of some vegetable life forms because a deliberate manipulation amounts to the decrease in total foliage number of an otherwise freely growing tree, thereby decreasing the total area of the tree capable of producing food for its life through photosynthesis and thus liberating oxygen which is so needed for the maintenance of the basic energy cycle in nature (Ghosh). Hence, Bonsai would go against the basic freedom of a tree to grow uninhibitedly, to go through its normal photosynthetic activity and be a member of the uninhibited energy cycle. Although trees are unable to speak about their freedom to grow uninhibitedly, we as conscious beings should do. Hence, Bonsai is essentially unethical as far as it is against the well-being of the vegetable life and ecological life as well (Ghosh and Nag).

The next argument from 'human likenesses' drawn from the basic welfaristic theory holds that a talk of freedom of plants should be based on a human parallel. So the morality and immorality of Bonsai may be decided by referring to 'what would happen to me' if I were in this situation? (Nag). Now if I put myself in a situation of a plant, being trimmed, dwarfed, chained, starved and so on, I would think it against my freedom to live uninhibitedly, to grow and to flourish. Hence, Bonsai is a case of going against the freedom of some life forms. It is against a perennial tree, which would go to 50-60 feet or even more. In this sense, it is undoubtedly unethical. Both Ghosh and Nag were aware of the counter arguments of the Bonsaist who argue that drawing on the same parallel, why at all should we consume vegetables. The stance of Ghosh and Nag was clarified further by holding that the ecological community is also a fine-tuned community where the existence of one is based on the other. Hence, our existence largely depends on what we consume from this community for we are unable to prepare our food. Although plants are able to prepare their own food, they also depend on carbon dioxide, water and sunlight for photosynthesis. In the energy cycle in nature, the balance of carbon dioxide depends largely on the release of the gas owing to animal activities like respiration, burning of hydrocarbons etc. So if do we not consume some vegetables, there will be perhaps no one to cry over ecological sustenance. So the question is, do we practice Bonsai for our basic sustenance? Does it in any way help maintaining the energy cycle, the balance of carbon dioxide and oxygen? It is important to use animate and inanimate things judiciously and not ruthlessly. Here arises the need of ecological sustenance as well as growth. Even utilitarians would argue in this manner. However, the welfarists would go further to speak of general well-being and not mere pleasure or happiness of human beings. Therefore, the welfarist has a final salvo at the Bonsaists accusing them as personal pleasure-seekers by arguing that the ideal of general welfare is not hampered by man consuming plants but it is really hampered by Bonsai practices. In fact what the Bonsaists think is that they are doing a benevolent job by restoring some plant species in an aesthetic way and some think that it is for the sake of the art that Bonsai is done. But to the welfarist antagonist, the work is not benevolent rather malevolent in so far as it is one way to hinder the natural growth of a plant thus depriving it of full flourish and photosynthetic activity causing ecological harm. Again the so-called art is not a healthy art at all for it is against the medium, i.e., the tree or the plant, and it is in fact essentially for the sake of the pleasure of the artist and not the art. Hence, Bonsai is unethical given the welfaristic standpoint.

It will be interesting to take on the other side of the welfarist argument immediately. I have already said that welfarism has been used differently by different people in this context, thanks to their capacity to find out what might follow from such first principle of morality. Professor Dayal and Professor Jain have no problem in accepting the scientific truths about energy cycle, energy balance, interdependence, and judicial use of animate and inanimate things. Where they differ is that although plants do not speak of their own rights and freedom, it is pointless even for us to harp of such populist sayings because,

(a) Plant life is destroyed naturally or accidentally as is with human beings (if we like the parallel) and we do not cry over their freedom and rights because it is but natural.

(b) Every plant or tree has to fight with nature for its growth from the stage of sowing (many seeds fall astray to decay), and we do not cry over the seeds which do not germinate though they had the right to grow.

(c) Therefore, it is a chance that a few trees grow to their potential and a few do not. However, this does not constitute their rights. Going by the protagonists' arguments, every vegetable and fruit should be allowed to grow to their optimum (for they should enjoy that freedom) before they are plucked and consumed.

(d) Thus there is no harm if some men of aesthetic sense give a new shape to trees and plants for it pleases not only the artist but the onlookers.

(d) In India Bonsai practice is negligible as per population ratio, so not alarming for ecological reasons. Hence, Bonsai should be accepted as an ethically desirable art form. It is also very useful in horticulture and botanical departments (Jain). To this it has been added that,

(f) Bonsai is an age long practice and not a recent one; it has the heritage to care plants, and any neglect shown to it reflects how unaware we are about a long-lived aesthetic practice and about the pragmatic value of this practice in the present scenario of dwindling plant species. We all have

> to be more conscious about caring and preserving important plant life in whatever way we can. Bonsai is one beautiful way to do so. Although, horticultural colleges need to be main centres of such practice, it should spread among people more and more. It is, therefore, one ethical art form (Dayal).

The inter-party feud among welfarists in this context appears to be an irresolvable imbroglio. If we have a look at someone trying to find out the logical strength and weakness of these arguments, it has to fall in the trap of committing another mistake because to weigh the logical strength of such informal arguments we do not have fixed parameters. It is better for an ethicist not to be involved in such things. However, as an ethical moderator, I pointed out the clear corroboration of views among these belligerent parties as far as both parties hold plants and trees ought to be used optimally for our basic sustenance. This was reinforced by the welfarists' (first group) next argument. They argued further that those who speak about complete lack of consciousness and the urge for growth in plants would reject their rights and freedom. It has been proved beyond doubt that plants do have inner urge to grow and have feelings. Hence, we should minimize their suffering as far as they do not have articulated language to protest or to demand something. This does not prevent us to realize that plants have finer feelings and urge when they are pruned, chained, cut and dwarfed. Therefore, we have to stop this unnecessary harm to plants for the sake of art, whatever degree of beauty may it create. Yet, if we have these life forms flourishing naturally, even then they look equally beautiful. Therefore, different Bonsai creations are at best imitations of the natural plant growth. Nevertheless, some horticultural, gardening and even logging practices are perfectly moral for they are for the welfare of the plant kingdom and for the entire community. So to cut a full-grown tree, to groom a tree from the cut offshoot is for the growth of a new life. This has not to be compared to cruelty to plants. Hence, although Bonsai is immoral, logging or some gardening practiced are not so (Nag).

Now the second group of welfarists as well as the Bonsaists would not go against the scientific truth that plants have feeling and that logging and some gardening practices are not comparable to

Bonsai practice. Therefore, there is no way whatsoever to accept that plants and trees are to be used for human welfare as well as general ecological welfare. There was also no doubt that the perennial tree is the main inspiration behind Bonsai and the perennial tree is more eco-friendly and useful. Nevertheless, that Bonsai is a negligible practice in India and that it also has some artistic and pragmatic value was gradually percolating among the participants. Another point surfaced gradually that among many human inspirations, artistic inspiration is one and it would be important to look into this aspect as well. However, this final point came gradually through the egoistic arguments of the Bonsaists.

(a) It was argued that the ethics-talk of Bonsai need not be man, nature and environment centred because man's aesthetic sense and his urge to experiment with styles to create an aesthetically beautiful environment for the aesthetic fulfilment of artists has to be taken into consideration as well.

(b) One has to accept that if optimum use of plants and trees are so important for human welfare, we cannot disregard one aspect of that welfare, viz., the fulfilment of human urge to create beautiful things with natural objects like plants.

(c) In fact, different people have different perspectives to evaluate the pragmatic value of plants and trees. One may be inclined to ruthlessly use it for income, which is immoral for it goes against the vegetable kingdom as such (readers may notice that there is a hidden welfarism within Bonsaists' egoism). Another may look at a plant as an item to decorate the household and yet another one to find out whether or not it is a monocot or a dicot. To a Bonsaist, however, a tree is an object of beauty and it may be experimented upon for different transformations to create to a fine piece of art. The human urge to transform ordinary things to a beautiful object is age old. Man has used things in this way and nothing is immoral in it, provided the whole race does not engage in only doing such things (readers may notice that there is a hidden warning for ruthless

Bonsai practice as well). So no doubt, the practice has to be judicious (Dey).

Now the platform of corroboration has been made more wider as we are ready to accept, (a) only pleasure satisfactions is not enough, (b) more Bonsai practice is not in favour of general welfare, (c) Bonsai is in India a low key affair, and (d) it has to be within limits. What is more important is to have perennial freely growing trees in India. Again, this final point gets most stress when we come to the pantheistic arguments. The pantheists appear to be heavily preoccupied with a divine presupposition. They have no doubt whatsoever that the entire existence is a divine transformation and as such, all existence is divine or that God is immanent in everything and presents everywhere. Every animate and inanimate objects are essentially valuable, possess intrinsic right to live freely and any intentional intervention may be a disrespect to the Divine. The simple argument holds that:

(a) Any cruel intervention in free plant growth will be in the long run devastating for the entire existence, Bonsai is one such intervention, and should be stopped (Singh).
(b) Man has no right to free play of whims against God and do whatever they like or do anything that satisfies or fulfils their ego like creating Bonsai (teachers of philosophy).
(c) The nature is like '*virāta purūṣa*' or a magnanimous divine person, the trees and plants being the parts of the *purūṣa*, without which it will be no more the same *purūṣa*. Any act of Bonsai practice to harm this divine existence, is immoral (Munda).

What are needed, therefore, in India are more flourishing trees for the natural balance as well as to return to the divine glory of nature (Singh and other teachers of philosophy). What is more interesting is to notice that the second group of welfarists and none of the Bonsaists were found objecting to this plain conclusion that "we do need more and more green cover in the form of more and more freely growing trees". Yet, the welfarists and the Bonsaists were not so vocal about either accepting or rejecting the pantheistic divinity of nature. They appeared to be silent regarding this matter for two reasons. One is that the botanists and the horticulturists (a mix of Marxists and secular scientists) were careful not to indulge themselves into hopeless religious dialogue. Second is that the Bonsaists did not find anything wrong with Bonsai even if the nature was divine. This takes us to the final argument of the egoists the argument from "pragmatics of art". The argument goes as follows:

(a) Even if the nature is divine essentially, a fine art like Bonsai is a form of worship of the nature because it is an attempt to create an aesthetically beautiful living thing and thus unfolding the inherent intellectual genius in man, who is also divine. The bone of contention is that the basic intention behind Bonsai is to unfold one's aesthetic genius through an object (tree). It is, therefore, moral (Chatterjee).

(b) To come to more pragmatic aspect of Bonsai we may hold that it does not go against plants or trees in anyway because it helps some species to grow either in a free space or in drawing rooms or in scant spaces in cities and towns just for the love of nature and plant life.

(c) In the rapidly urbanized India, we just cannot go back to the old times. This is a fact that vacant space has run out and is running out rapidly. Therefore, we should be more practical in using whatever space we have at our disposal now. Bonsai is one nice way to use scant space available to us for gardening, which is eco-friendly, as well as fulfilling to the art loving people. It is thus moral (Sengupta).

(d) Bonsai as a fine art is different from other fine arts as far as our resources are quite limited. At best, we have seeds and germinating plants, which we have to care everyday for its growth. With this, our urge to care and to create grows and it gradually turns out to be a beautiful object. However, for this we need a sense of '*Rasa*' or 'aesthetic feeling'. So Bonsai need not be evaluated merely on its use or pragmatics, it has to be evaluated on the basis of aesthetic enjoyment or '*Rasa bodh*' (Chatterjee).

Whatever it may be, the final pragmatic argument does reflect the fact that the Bonsaists are ready to accept that although it would have been more practical to have more freely growing green cover, the growing urbanization allows us to practice Bonsai at least in towns and cities, but not in all available village space. With the acceptance that in India, it should have a more or less restricted use, is clear. The question is whether it is pragmatic to have Bonsai practice in village as well, which still forms 70 per cent of India? Here the Bonsaists are stressing to transcend the use and practicability of Bonsai to look more deeply into the age-old human urge to create and experiment while creating beautiful things.

Where we now stand is that irrespective of the value of perennial trees and more green cover, the fact that India is already heavily urbanized and deforested, we need to be more eco-conscious and one way is to try new ways to use even scanty space available to us in an aesthetically beautiful way. Therefore, it appears that we are heading towards a consensus that "granted the truth that we need more flourishing trees, wherever we enjoy that legacy, however, we do need urban culture to care for trees, and it is for that we need Bonsai". Again, "granted that in India we have been doing much for the primal forests, it is time to be more serious at the institutional level, like in horticultural colleges to find out new ways to protect plant species". But then the fact is that everybody in towns and cities and in horticultural colleges may not have the time, the expertise and the fund (enough I think) to practice Bonsai, it has to be a restricted affair and not necessarily following all the intricacies and process basic to Bonsai practice. Protection of depleting plant species is possible in other scientific ways as well.

Naturally, therefore, the corroborative spirit of the house was reflected in these words of Dr. Nag, "Looking at the present need, Bonsai may turn out to be a necessity, even if we are not so immaculate in artistic practices. The usable land area is fast depleting in India and one feels that in the end we may not think to ban this practice of Bonsai. There can be no law to ban Bonsai for it will ever remain a pragmatic horticultural practice and a limited aesthetic practice among negligible urban populace in India. It may turn out to be one useful way to nurture dwindling plant varieties. For its dwarfed stature, the works may be stored at plenty and cared in museums in horticultural colleges. It may turn out to be attractive for theoretical and practical purposes for the botanists and horticulturists. We may learn a lot from the different genetic make-up of Bonsai and know how they would grow normally. However, a tree is a tree; we all have a complex interactive relationship with it. Let us be more concerned with growing perennial trees". (Nag on behalf of the house)

It was, however, a more or less not so comfortable affair for the pantheists but then we do not live in a fully God intoxicated India, and their presupposition needs careful examination first before their arguments may be taken seriously. Even if the nature is not accepted to be divine, we can take careful steps to restore the benign beauty of nature. Even if we are not God—intoxicated, we can still be serious nature lovers. Now we have at hand another serious moral argument. If the presupposition of pantheistic ethics need a careful look, why not have a closer look at welfarism and egoism as well, which were active in the consensus anyway? We may now leave our ethics students and teachers to ponder over such questions, with a caution however, that only doing such things will not be doing applied ethics. The fact is that the common person participating in the dialogue did not care for the theoretical and analytical work any more. If we, the ethicists, take this task further, do we think that we will decide for ever the value of one ethical theory over other theories in case of resolving moral impasse like this one? If we think so, we shall fall in the trap of ethical engineering which is not applying ethics. Anyway, for all academic purposes we may continue in ethics with the debate that whether or not the justification of environmental rights would depend on religious or quasi-religious presuppositions and not on non-religious presuppositions.

However, I am more interested in performing my final task *qua* applied ethicist. I have to filter out those decision-making rules, which the house suggested along with those suggested by other people with regard to Bonsai practice in India. The rules have been pronounced as follows:

(1) Looking at the moral and the cultural background of India as well as the available land for forestation, more stress has to be given to the plantation of a variety of trees. This takes precedence over any other practice like Bonsai or even social forestation.

(2) Even if gardening is ecologically and aesthetically beneficial, Bonsai may be taken seriously as a useful form

of gardening and not a mere pastime of a wealthy few in urban societies.

(3) For this, Bonsai art has to spread among other people through some education or other means. Scientists and Bonsai lovers should find ways to raise Bonsais at a low cost among common people.

(4) People should be educated about its scientific and pragmatic value rather than its aesthetic value.

(5) Bonsai need not be raised as religious necessity nor should it be prevented or banned on religious grounds for it has definite scientific, ecological and social values.

(6) Nevertheless, Bonsai should be practiced at a limited scale giving way to plantation of more and more trees. It should be practiced more in horticultural colleges and botanical departments and societies.

(7) Students of schools and colleges should be taken to Bonsai museums for a first hand knowledge of the different species of rare plants and trees. They should be educated about how to raise a Bonsai.

(8) Barring students of fine arts, students specializing in Bonsai art and few amateurs of great interest, Bonsai as pure art form need not be taken too seriously among the masses. Even not so artistic and not so stylistic Bonsais may serve the main purpose of creating banks of plant species.

(9) Regular Bonsai exhibition-cum-training sessions ought to be held in Agriculture colleges and other places all over India and details of its social and ecological value to be projected clearly to the masses.

Now the readers should notice that these are not fixed set of moral rules like divine rules, which need not change. Further discussion and corroboration may change them to a great extent or to some extent. However, every time our ethically charged people need moral debates to do so. Thus, we have to care for moral debates, corroboration and decision-making rules if we want to engage in what we call applying ethics. We also find that our ethicists do have a role to play as far as they act anchor to moral debates, they act corroborators, and then participate in elaborate post-corroboration analysis, which is purely technical and unique to a trained mind. The findings of such analysis is of great academic value no doubt and only when we feel that this should spread to the non-philosophers, teaching theoretical ethics to non-philosophers become important. Only then do we have to reconsider the way we should teach ethics, including applied ethics. I would consider this issue in the next chapter.

NOTES

1. Chan, Peter, "*Bonsai Master Class*", Paul Press, London, 1987.
2. Shin-ichi Anzai quotes Muso Soseki in his paper "*Is the World a Garden? Garden Aesthetics between the Japanese and English Traditions*". This appears in his paper presented in the XII International Congress of Aesthetics in Tokyo, Japan, 2001, p. 6.

5

Models of Teaching Ethics including Applied Ethics

We have seen at least three important things by this time with regard to applied ethics. First, applied ethics is within ethics properly so called. Second, applied or practical ethics has intimate relation with professional life. Finally, applied ethics calls for a proper model of application of ethics, which, I believe is inter-subjective corroboration. This last finding is important for us in so far as a misconception regarding methodology of ethical application leads us to a complete confusion about applied ethics itself because we do not understand properly what is applied by whom and why in applied ethics. The confusion we have seen is credited to deductivism and inductivism, and what is interesting is, both models beg *teaching ethics* in applying ethics. We have to take up this issue now. Does ethical application necessarily demand ethics teaching? If yes, we have to answer why such teaching is needed. Who is expected to teach and to whom? In addition, most importantly, what has to be taught in ethics course and how? However, in course of our earlier analysis of deductivism and inductivism, we have noticed that the supporters of ethical chauvinism does uphold the view that ethics teaching is an integral part of ethical application because without the knowledge of at least one ethical standard (the knowledge imparted by ethics experts), no ordinary men in professional life would be able to resolve ethical impasse. The ethics *gurus* are capable of ethical resolution like experts in that field and act consultants by virtue of such normative ethical knowledge (which they have been taught by their *gurus*). Therefore, applying ethics does beg teaching of theoretical ethics, particularly normative theories. We may say that ethical engineering in any form begs ethics teaching by ethics experts. I have dealt in details the absurdities and fallacies underlying such a project of ethical application. I have also justified why normative ethical teaching alone would not do justice to ethics teaching. However, it is time now to take up these questions of teaching in more details in the context of ethical application for two reasons. First, we shall come to know about some such models of ethical teaching within ethical engineering, which, however, as an anti-climax is deemed to be unjustified. Second, we shall come to know the proper model of ethics teaching including teaching applied ethics. This second assertion may raise a few eyebrows because properly understood, applied ethics even in the sense in which I have spoken of, does open some scope for theoretical ethics and ethics teaching. Then why blame the other party? In fact, what I propose to justify is not that teaching ethics is needed for artificial ethical resolution of value-laden problems of practical urgency but for undertaking the task of intersubjective corroboration. Nevertheless, this will not satisfy the critics because they have reasons to doubt that even if applying ethics follows intersubjective corroboration, then at the stages of framing questionnaire, arranging a dialogue and moderating it and at the stage of the corroboration analysis, ethics teaching is need for all interested parties (philosophers and non-philosophers).

Skeptics' fresh sets of doubts need a careful treatment. Let me be very clear about application of ethics. First, ethical application needs a definite value-laden practical problem for resolution (no one supplies it to an expert). Second, preferably ethicists or a person trained in ethics is entrusted to prepare a questionnaire and select professionals and other parties for a moral dialogue resulting to a moral resolution of the value-laden problem. Further, decision-making rules are clearly stated for the professionals in their fields so that they may take practical decisions having a moral face. Finally, we have to undertake an analysis of the moral arguments and moral views of the participants in a moral dialogue to find out the practical value of normative theories. Clearly, the *second* and the *final* tasks *within* the entire applied ethical exercise are of great importance. The second task, namely, the preparation of questionnaire for a moral dialogue demand sound knowledge of theoretical ethics because one has to put ethically oriented questions to bring out the moral opinions of the debating parties. Even during the debate, a sound knowledge of ethics is needed for moderating the dialogue or even pointing out the apparent fallacies in view. The final task is indubitably theory based because a post-corroboration analysis of the moral opinions and moral arguments demand sound knowledge of theoretical ethics. Hence, theoretical ethics has to play a vital role within applied ethics. Moreover, to say that applied ethics stops where ethical resolution is arrived at is a clear confusion about what I have said. So to say, that the stage of resolution is primary and the post-corroboration stage secondary is not to commit that applied ethics is without post-corroboration analysis. Rather, it is very much within it, and to be emphatic, there is no applied ethics without post-corroboration analysis. Even then we come to know that there is no apparent confusion in what I have said because even if in the second stage, knowledge of theoretical ethics does become prominent in ethical application (which stage is primary), it does not amount to the same as what critics have in mind, that is, at this stage, we apply ethical theories artificially. Neither should the deductivists and the inductivists be enthusiastic about finding a fault in my opinion to support their cause because in stage two, knowledge of ethics is in no way a means to resolve ethical impasse by one or more ethics experts. Rather, ethicists and/or non-ethicists interested in application of ethics use their ethical knowledge to prepare a questionnaire and moderate a moral dialogue, which, clearly means to initiate a moral dialogue to encourage agreements and disagreements and to reach a climax gradually by coming to a probable resolution. There is thus a difference between using one or more normative theories by one or more ethics experts (to rule out non-ethicist experts) artificially to resolve a moral crises at the second stage on the one hand and on the other hand to justify theoretical need in ethical application and using normative ethical knowledge along with metaethical and practical ethical knowledge to prepare a tool for moral debate resulting to moral resolution. In the second instance, theoretical ethics is not applied in the *direct* sense of the term in which the deductivists and the inductivists understand it. Hence, applied ethics does not stop at the second stage or that applied ethics is just this. It is something more. It is a return to theoretical ethics to make the task of practical ethics complete at the final stage or the post-corroboration stage. Yes, there is no doubt that the knowledge of theoretical ethics at least indirectly helps the ethicist-moderator (which may include non-philosophers) in a moral resolution. Nevertheless, this is only a part of applying ethics, an important or primary part, not the whole of application of ethics. Therefore, in no sense do we say that in intersubjective corroboration we fall in the same trap of application of theoretical ethics artificially by an ethics expert (philosophers so to say).

To ask the question more directly, do we not need the knowledge of theoretical ethics at any stage whatsoever? Yes, we do need it along with the knowledge of metaethics, in the second and final stages. Therefore, it will be a blunder to think that ethicists or interested parties in ethical application need to be trained only in normative ethics. We shall come to the details at a proper place. I will also try to justify that even at stage four, that is, the post-corroboration analysis, a mere training of normative ethics would not do. There is no doubt that wholesome academic training in ethics does matter within applied ethics but the training does not amount to teaching about norms and ways to apply them. In fact, such training is not only needed for the philosophers or ethicists; it is needed for other parties interested in ethical application. Next, such training in academic ethics is not for artificial application for ethical resolution. Further, such training may be a continuous process within a civilized democratic society to enrich the moral vocabulary of the non-philosophers and, therefore, ethics teaching and training may be largely an interdisciplinary programme as well but that does not mean that we have to teach academic ethics necessarily across the curriculum. It does not amount to have centres of ethics consultancy and to send professionals mandatory for a normative ethics teaching. It does not amount to normative teaching mandatory in schools and colleges either. A training and educative task like this one has to be voluntary and particularly needed for those indulging in the task of ethical corroborator and not for those who participate in ethical debates because debating does not beg theory cooption. It is not a healthy affair. It is, therefore, not mandatory in a civil society for all to become ethical corroborators but it may be desirable in a civil society for us to participate in moral dialogues for ethical resolution of value-laden problems. Hence, the entire course of wholesome teaching and training in ethics is for those active participants in applying ethics who assume the role of moderators-corroborators and not for the entire civil population. It is rather a day dream and even foolish to go for a theory cooption for the population because this may lead us nowhere. Interestingly corroborators need to be more careful about theory cooption for that may end up in ethical engineering and not intersubjective corroboration, the former being a misconceived application of ethics. This may be a little annoying for those who have loved to see ethics teaching and training go global for ethically acting, deciding and resolving. Let us come finally to those people who speak of teaching ethics for an artificial application of ethics. Let us also come to the models they propound. According to ethical engineering, we may speak of two models of ethics teaching and training for a common purpose, namely, enabling people to apply ethics, which, I have said is misconceived. For the sake of discussion, we may classify these models as the *sophistical and the casuistic models of ethics teaching and training*. We shall come to know later on that for the sake of simplicity, these models may be put under the "sophistical model". We shall also come to know that the deductivists and the inductivists have been the chief proponents of these models of ethics teaching for that clearly suits their scheme of ethical engineering. However, for all this we have to know about the justifications for teaching ethics and for the models they propose for teaching ethics. However, one should keep in mind that ethics teaching and training may have other purposes as well. As I have said, it may be needed for participating as an ethics corroborator and analyst in ethical application, it may be needed for students and teachers of philosophy, especially those specializing in the field of ethics and it may be needed for those non-philosophers who neither participate as corroborators and analysts nor specializes in ethics rather, are pre-professionals interested in inter-disciplinary courses for their academic and social value. The first group of students of ethics is thus having a 'predominant practical aim' rather than a purely academic one. The second group of students of ethics has a 'predominant academic aim' rather than a practical aim. The third group of students of ethics has more of an aim of 'inter-disciplinary study' rather than an urge for in-depth ethics studies and an urge for participating in a practical effort. Interesting is to notice that the first group of students of ethics are those having more or less sound knowledge of wholesome ethics and a social commitment towards participating in the process of application of ethics notwithstanding the fact that they are not ethical engineers. However, the post-corroboration analysis done by them does contribute much to academic ethics. The second group of students may likely have more or less sound knowledge of wholesome ethics (we cannot be sure of it as it wholly depends on the course they are taught at different places by different people) for they just have an academic taste. These students have to be watched for their decision taken (while they study ethics or after finishing a satisfactory course) regarding whether or not they participate in a practical ethical venture as has been done by the students of the first group. However, it is a misconception that a continuous study of theoretical ethics has become redundant for the people of the first group and those in the second group. It is clear that participating in practical ethical venture is quite different from receiving wholesome training in ethics including practical ethics because a mere knowledge of value-laden issues, their resolution and the analysis of the practical value of normative theories within practical ethics is purely theoretical in so far as the receiver of such education along with normative and metaethics teaching does not enter into the actual *act of corroboration, resolution and analysis*. When this practical interest is shown, education of ethics including practical ethics is complete. This will be my main contention when I proceed to analyze the pros and cons of different models of ethics education. Therefore, the people of second group are likely to be handicapped by such practical act within ethics education and are thus not being educated in wholesome ethics. Nevertheless, so called ethics educated persons belonging to any of these groups may start acting an ethical engineer if and only if the person has been taught of a practical ethics, which is ethical engineering. This is true for the third group as well because mainly pre-professionals receiving either a wholesome or partial ethics education would act an engineer, provided they have been taught like that. I think, they have been taught ethics (either partly or wholly) in a sophistical way. Whereas my contention is to show that sophistry in ethics teaching is either *pure pedagogy* or *anagogy* or both, which is truly speaking neither teaching wholesome ethics nor teaching practical ethics rather teaching ethical engineering. It will be clear as we proceed that both pure pedagogy and anagogy or what is sophistry in ethics education has been responsible for the growth of deductivism and inductivism in practical ethics.

Let us come to the details of these models of ethics teaching (including teaching practical ethics). Christopher Gill in "Greek Ethics: Overview" explains that 'with the widespread professionalism in the field of knowledge and education, some influential Athenians in fifth century B.C. were enthusiastic about teaching the art of rhetoric, debate, arguments and so on by accepting fee. These teachers of skills were the sophists and their occupation, sophistry, which, however, were strongly challenged for such mindless act by Aristophanes and Plato. The main point of such criticism was whether or not the authority of imparting education and spreading knowledge belonged to an expert or experts who were expected to do the job most ably and unfalteringly'. Another point of criticism was whether or not ethical values ought to be spread in the community and ethical crises resolved in the community by an expert or experts who were expected to do these jobs most ably and unfalteringly. So the problem is, is it proper to bestow complete authority to expert or experts in education, particularly ethics education? In addition, is it proper to give full authority to expert or experts regarding resolving moral crisis? Christopher Gill in his essay "Greek Ethics: Overview" comments: "This debate is analogous with one of those associated in modern times with 'applied ethics', namely that of the relationship between professional expertise and the ethical standards of the community".[1] What Gill means by 'the ethical standards of the community' is, 'the moral pluralism with regard to a social concern for ethical resolution of value-laden practical problems'. Plato's concern for a role of the community as such in practical ethical matters is clear when we find him asking Protagoras about the role of the expert sophist in public debate about ethical values. Plato would imagine a very limited but important role of an ethics teacher in such community situation because such teachers are at best facilitators of ethical debates and resolution and not preachers of values and virtues. In fact, values and virtues cannot be taught so artificially to people and ethical problems cannot be so artificially resolved. Plato has the same concern about methodology in ethical application when in Gorgias he questions the ethical validity of moral teaching and preaching, and also moral dialogues with skilled masters of ethics. The criticism is also directed at the validity of even moral debates and moral rhetorics pointlessly to resolve a crisis because these methods should not be applied where they are completely misunderstood as belonging to the authority of skilled masters. Sophistry in a different form may be found in the Hippocratic age, particularly in the field of medicine. Here the expert doctors, assuming moral authority in matters of value-laden issues in medicine assumed the task of the sophists to resolve trifling value-laden matters. The moral guideline in form of an oath was put forward by Hippocrates to be universally accepted code in medical profession, which was thought to be the only standard of ethicality in that profession. It was far from the public debate in which doctors are one party to ethical resolution.

What was unique during the age of the Greek sophists like Protagoras, Thrasymachus, Gorgias and others, and also during the age of sophists in medicine, was to evolve a method of such debates and persuasion by experts that it were a science (Plato calls it a pseudo-science) of ethical resolution. This was done in a democratic set-up although which was indubitably less of "truth tracking" than "power tracking" says Robert Nozick because such debates were not merely arranged and moderated by these sophists, the expert in ethics, they enforced their morals through it for a universal acceptance. This is the ethical chauvinism and engineering by what one knows to be absolutely true. It is a matter of power of one's theoretical knowledge that the "other party" has been completely subdued in a moral dialogue and moral resolution. Moreover, all this was done for the sake of preparing "ethically charged good citizens". These good citizens came to their *gurus* for wisdom and to learn the art of good living. These experts were according to Plato the corruptors of youth (mostly aristocratic) as they laid much stress on how to win over opponent in a moral debate and moral resolution rather than corroborating, learning and finding the truth. The approach of the experts is one of an emotion manipulator rather than a moderator of rational discourse. This emotive win of the manipulators and the unnatural self-satisfaction, which they have in moral dialogue, results into pleonexia or a pathological desire to have more. Hence, the ethical engineers or the moral sophists are pleonastic people who want to show people that by virtue of their moral knowledge and moral authority they have won the game. This predatory disposition in man is but natural accepts Hobbes, and what he forgot to mention is that all this is unethical. Ethical sophism is thus a model of teaching ethics in which on the one hand we have ethics teachers or experts having enough theoretical knowledge of ethics and on the other hand ordinary ethicsless people awaiting such moral knowledge to dawn on them. These teachers hope to teach the "art of moral behaviour" to ordinary people, may be through a dialogue but in that dialogue, the teacher send surmises and the disciples receive them unchallenged. First, do ethical sophists have wholesome knowledge of ethics? No, because wholesome knowledge of ethics includes indulging in practical ethical venture, which is not artificial application of ethical theories to resolve moral problems as, thinks the sophists in their engineering effort. Rather, wholesome knowledge of ethics is knowledge of normative ethics, metaethics, theoretical aspects of practical ethics and indulging in ethical application in the capacity of a corroborator and analyst of moral dialogue. Hence, the sophistical model of teaching is most likely to miss the points that teaching ethics includes teaching metaethics, theoretical aspects of applied ethics and most importantly, to get involved in a practical venture. However, none of the above things can be learnt and taught to its full extent. That is not a great drawback natural limitation. Next, the sophistical model of teaching tends to forget that there can be no art of teaching moral behaviour to ordinary people or even people having some knowledge of ethics because what is "moral behaviour" is not well defined to all of us. Experts think that they have a complete and absolute knowledge of morally behaving and thus have the authority to teach such things to ordinary people. Finally, the sophistical model of ethics teaching is completely at loss in thinking that ethics teaching is needed for the sophists or the ethical experts or ethical engineers because they alone have the moral authority to apply ethics in the worldly situations, and whatever teaching of ethics they are giving to the ordinary people is not really to find a truth or let know about a truth or to let people apply ethics themselves but to overpower with their moral authority. Even if the experts thought that the ordinary people would resolve ethical crisis after ethical teaching, it is another misconception as nothing but the buck of moral engineering has been passed to fresh set of sophists. The sophistical model appears to have no clue to teach ethics to the people because all ordinary people cannot and need not be taught ethics. Even if we undertake such a gigantic but foolish task, the model does not mention to teach "what" in ethics. Moreover, it forgets that not all people can recall from their knowledge repository the befitting norm for moral resolution. Therefore, let us conclude that sophistical model fails to answer the important questions regarding teaching ethics and practical ethics, and has to be avoided therefore. Nevertheless, the sophists have to say something in favour of their proposed model of ethics teaching. Most of them would be happy with what is known as *indoctrination* or the method of teaching morality by an expert teacher that attempts at influencing pupils, mostly of school level to adopt moral values on the basis of what has been imbibed by the teacher because he or she assumes an unquestioning moral authority. In other words, "indoctrination" is a sophistical model of teaching ethics (particularly in schools) which is a one-way-traffic. The teacher goes on spreading gems of ethical values to shape, guide and form moral values in their morally blank pupils so that they believe that they have done a great national duty in ethically charging the future of the nation. (The teachers are likely to take some fees for that). But the situation is not so comical thinks R.M. Hare as he hopes that it would be a little foolish that we as parents and as teachers will never intervene in influencing children's moral growth because we think that they must find their own morality. Now this necessary intervention is not sophistry because "we cannot help influencing our children; the only question is, how, and in what direction".[2] But what is interesting is to notice that teachers are just important members in the environment influencing necessarily the moral attitude of children. Therefore, we have to allow that children necessarily acquire moral attitudes from their environment, which includes parents and teachers. Parents and teachers are not the only authorities or only responsible people who may be bestowed the task of moral education because equally true is that "we cannot help prevent the society in which we live, the masses, other children, other adults, and even different political, religious, economical and biological factors influencing the moral growth in children. I have already said in an earlier discussion that we being the members of ecological community are definitely receiving moral education from a number of sources. The only difference is that the other sources do not educate us in the same way as teachers and parents educate us or even the way in which the church and the priests educate us. Why "to educate" is only "to be taught by an expert" is not known to us. Does education beg a mere classroom or home-type confined teaching in lessons or sermons? More appropriately asked, "Do we mean to say that to educate in moral values through indoctrination is what the only meaning of moral education is?" An additional question is, "is it a special form of pedagogy that helps inculcate moral values?"

R.M. Hare should not be misunderstood here. What he means to say is that environmental factors including parental and teacher's behaviours and surmises does influence child's moral growth apart from other influencing factors but he is wrong in so far as he thinks that a child cannot find its own morality—it is "obviously absurd", he says. Then the conclusion is, children cannot "find their own morality", and indoctrination is necessary. We have a blatant confusion between the child's mind being filled with rudimentary notions of examples of good and bad behaviour owing to parental, teacher's and other influences and the child's mind seeking ethical education through a critical acumen. Here is confusion that ethics education to children is pure pedagogy, the most responsible parties being the teachers—the sermonizers, whose authority is unchallenged. This pedagogy is sophistical, and this is what we are trying to refute. Yet, the message inherent in such criticism is that adults should not act sophists to deliberately attempt at shaping and controlling child's moral character. There should not be a deliberate attempt to influence by commenting on or indicating what child's attitude should be towards other random environmental influences at work.

Here another problem creeps in. The question is, is it possible to allow random environmental influences by not at all controlling them in whatever circumstances? Then we have to imagine that at one stage in child's life, it should be allowed to behave dishonestly and immorally within an environmental influence before he or she has come to realize what is right and good. Moreover, another problem is actually, a child would first grow freely in environment and then learn what should be done in a restricted condition. This is an imaginary empirical claim and may not be supported easily by evidences. Even if we cite instances of "free schools", we forget that pupils there are in control of adults, and adults do intervene in the lopsided moral behaviours of the children. We cannot cite an instance of an orphan in an orphanage either who without an adult control has "found his morality" in the imaginary way explained above. Therefore, what do we say about indoctrination and pedagogy now? Robin Barrow asks: "And the reality is that, whether we like it or not, most of us as teachers have to deal with children who have already begun the process of acquiring behaviour patterns and embryonic values which may as a matter of fact strike us as objectionable and which may as a matter of fact be there to stay if something is not done about them. It really is absurdly improbable to suggest that everyone would be a saint if only teachers would shut up".[3] Is it true that our attempt to criticize moral pedagogy in a sophistical manner should be understood in the way Barrow have understood?

I don't find anything objectionable in Barrow's demand of allowing teachers to intervene in moral matters and his basic support to Hare that a child has to be helped initially every now and then about moral matters. In addition, we know that these moral matters are not very grave ones like whether or not euthanasia is good or bad rather, things like what is bad in spitting and pissing in classrooms. May be older boys in school need more important moral interventions like, what is bad in carrying a gun in a classroom and so on. However, question is, does Barrow realize as a teacher that there is clear difference between teaching ethics or moral philosophy and morality, moral codes, ethical codes, socially acceptable moral norms etc.? What I was criticizing is not indoctrination is cases of imbibing moral values in children but a pure pedagogy in schools where ethics or moral philosophy has been taught to school children through the method of indoctrination or in this case, I call it sophistical pedagogy. We have to realize as teachers that in schools we have to face a situation of teaching not common morality but ethics, and here indoctrination or pure pedagogy does not help nor is it desirable because that is moral chauvinism of teachers. This will then hamper the analytic skill and urge of pupils to receive ethics education. The moot issue is that whether or not the model of indoctrination is in any way pragmatic and desirable in ethics education in schools. We may extend this to ask, whether the same holds in college education as well? Therefore, our problem is to find out a sound model of teaching ethics in our educational institutions. One interesting issue may be, whether or not it is desirable to teach ethics in our schools at any level because that may be overdoing in so far as ethics teaching (if it is wholesome) is something not at all possible at the school level. Moreover, every teaching programme must have a well-defined goal. What ought to be the desirable goal of teaching academic ethics in our schools (let us allow it for high school students at least)? Do our revered sophists think that teaching a course of ethics would prepare ethically charged citizens who later on join the masses to resolve moral crises? If they think like that, it is moral engineering, against which I have been arguing. Let us think coolly whether it is sufficient for our school students to indoctrinate in common morality, socially acceptable norms and to some extent noble virtues? Yes, this is possible only if our students, at least some of them, show signs of lopsided behaviour, or do we have to go for some such surmises even if our pupils are behaving perfectly well. Many problems arise here. Even if we start teaching about the value of some moral virtues to our students, is it not necessary to encourage them in participating in an examination of those absolute virtues like friendship? Is it not desirable for us to invite at least our older students in schools to find out whether or not friendship is absolutely morally good? If we start encouraging such things, I hope it is no more indoctrination or pure pedagogy. So, two-way traffic in teaching virtues to students may be allowed. Thus, an intervention model giving more liberty to our teachers may not be ethical either.

Another interesting question is, is it desirable to intervene through an expert in teaching religious values in our schools? This is more crucial when such religious teachings takes the form of moral science and is often confused with moral teaching or even teaching ethics. The problem is grave when we consider it in the context of a democracy like India, which also claims (constitutionally) to be a secular democracy. The problem is, who is expected to teach which religion and to whom? Some people think that this is a question in a bad taste. We can teach things like religious values and not religion. For instance, we may send a few sermons to our students in schools about God's creative act, that is, the world is in fact divine, all beings low and high are divine and to be loved as ourselves and so on. First, we have to be careful that neither our teachers nor students are necessarily theists in a secular society. We may be doing a great harm by preaching such things in the name of moral and ethical teaching because a Buddhist, a Jain teacher and student may not like such things. So why teach them? Why intervene? Why preach religious values in the name of moral teaching? Hence, sophistical anagogy, the indoctrination in another form, the religions one, has to be carefully avoided as a model of teaching ethics.

Both "pure pedagogy" and "anagogy" in school ethics education is thus hopeless. It may be a matter of serious concern as I have said that even an attempt at wholesome ethics education and pseudo-ethical education is objectionable in schools. Therefore, we do not find much value in indoctrination or on a sophist spreading absolute values. When we reflect coolly even about indoctrination in case of imbibing a particular moral value or religious value or both to be absolutely true, we may soon find that with age, the whole affair turns out to be distasteful because it is detrimental to the budding ethical analysts' critical mind. Barrow appears to have thought coolly finally, to say "we must influence children's moral development, because we cannot help so doing. We cannot do better than influence them towards acceptance of those values that we regard as most reasonable. However, if we are to avoid indoctrination we must seek ultimately to cultivate an open mind on the question. For any institution such as a school will enshrine various values, and if we wish to make a positive attempt to combat the danger of indoctrination we must have them out in the open and be prepared to talk about them".[4] He, therefore, rejects his zeal to support "unquestionable indoctrination" model of teaching ethics (it appears) as he accepts that "And yet we cannot meaningfully discuss fundamental questions such as the universalizability of moral judgements, or the question of whether considerations of harm are necessarily relevant to moral debate, with children, at least until the stage of secondary education. It is essential, therefore, that at the primary stage reasons should be given where they can be, so that children acquire the notion that the beliefs and behavioural patterns that they are gradually coming to adopt are supposed to be based on reason than on the dictates of authority, and that at the secondary stage those reasons themselves should be subjected to critical examination".[5] What is most interesting is to notice that finally Barrow recognizes the fact that ethics teaching through sophistical model of "indoctrination"[6] in school is an absurd proposition. He says, "An open mind in the moral sphere involves recognizing this problem (no absolute indoctrination is possible). In addition, to undertake an inquiry into this problem is to do moral philosophy. Therefore, a necessary antidote to moral indoctrination is an introduction to moral philosophy provided that nobody is so foolish as to assume that what a moral philosopher says is the case must be the case"[7] So he joins us to uphold the truth that sophistical model of ethical teaching is too absurd and a sophistical model of value teaching should be carefully avoided as well.

Now 'value' has become a new *mantra* in philosophical and non-philosophical circles in India. Many western countries have been harping on it for quite some time now. Almost all concerned people in India are talking about the value of value-teaching or value-oriented teaching in our schools and colleges. These people are concerned about teaching values to all and not only to the philosophy students. The main reason is that educators and policy-makers have suddenly come to realize that there is a widespread degradation in human character because there is a degradation in education, an education which is value-neutral and not value-oriented. Many people in India think that this degradation in education is due to the barbaric mercantile model of education in India initiated by Macaulay and cared and encouraged by post-independent policy-makers. In the name of sophistical pedagogy we have corroded basic Indian value oriented education. We have eliminated arts, philosophy, spiritual education, *yoga, dharma,* our cultural heritage, perennial mathematics, history everything. Let us look at what Professor Murli Manohar Joshi, our Union Human Resource Development Minister says in one of his inaugural lectures: "What has been lost in terms of pedagogy and richness of contents of knowledge and skills has still not been remedied".[8] So to find out remedy, he calls us to think about the 'kind of education' to be promoted. The kind is clearly, 'value-oriented education'. But what is 'value-oriented education'? And what is 'value-orientedness'? He goes on giving examples first (pp. 9-10), the education of the *gurukula*, Swami Dayananda Saraswati's and Swami Vivekananda's man making education (basically Vedāntic); the Gandhian education (the training of the hand, heart, non-violence, self-control) and Tagore's education in nature that gradually promotes the religion of man. Prof. Joshi also reminds us of Bankim Chandra's '*Bande Mātaram*' and Aurobindo Gosh's 'superhumanity' and calls for a complete transformation of our educational system. Now we have to read between the lines to find out what he means about 'values' in education. He actually speaks of 'spiritual and religious values' and all examples cited above reminds us of teaching the religious values propagated in the *Vedas*. the *Vedānta* and by *neo-Vedāntins*. So we must not have any doubt about which values to be taught in our education. Let us remember that he may be demanding such value education across-the-curriculum because this can make us people of noble characters. However, all this has to be taught by the teachers not in the old pedagogic fashion we have been carrying so far rather, it has to be a more interactive one, following the *gurukula* system so to say. But even then an omnipotent torch-bearer of such value-wisdom shall sermonize, shall indoctrinate and propagate values to obedient pupils. The teacher has to teach the 'art' of a value-guided living. Complete sophistry is at hand. To make it more clear, he writes (p. 15), "advancement of knowledge demands methods by which knowledge can be summed up and possessed in a state of self-possession. Value-oriented education should ultimately issue from and result in the knowledge of what can be described as all-embracing Self and Universal Reality".[9] So the method should be such that it ultimately leads academia the knowledge of the Ultimate Reality, and he is very emphatic that "science, like philosophy, grasps the nature of the Ultimate Reality".[10] He then goes on cumbersomely to let us know what Ultimate Knowledge of Ultimate Reality is! It is "to develop among all the highest Goodwill".[11] It is clear that our new sophistical pedagogy ensuing from the value-charged teachers and passed on to valueless pupils be in a manner such that the teachers are able to do only one thing, that is, to let pupils know about what this Highest Goodwill is and how to inculcate this in one's character. This value-education seems to be complete through a new pedagogy or more appropriately, anagogy or *sophistical anagogy* because only one basic education has to ensue in *gurukula* type pedagogy, viz., 'the value of becoming a spiritually soaked person—a person who has hopefully realized the Ultimate Reality'. Although our professor was careful not to give a name to this Reality but it is understandable. This is a great tragedy because what value–education has amounted to in the name of shaping great moral character or in the name of ethically training a person is *Vedāntic* value-education. All teaching will be thus hopeless if the taught has no idea about a supreme metaphysical Reality. This sophistical anagogy is another intervention in a secular set-up to teach religious and spiritual values. Moreover, if it were not in the name of ethical values, and in reality in the name of values in general, how do we imagine that our task has been completed? Who would imagine that value teaching does not take care of material values, secular values, environmental values and many others? But value teaching is a different teaching—teaching wholesome axiology, and that too in our schools and colleges. This is really difficult, may be a little overestimating but it is not as immoral as imagining to impart spiritual education to the entire masses through anagogy to make them morally charged. So let us be careful about 'sophistical anagogy' as well. We shall find later on that the 'casuistic model' of teaching values, even ethical values, is in reality anagogical in nature and thus sophistical. But we shall now consider here the two most widespread sophistical models—pure pedagogy or indoctrination and anagogy or religious—spiritual indoctrination. Let us clarify first of all that there is no impure pedagogy. "Pure pedagogy" is to stress the fact that it is a model of teaching ethical values and morality in the name of 'ethics education' in a way such that an ethical expert champions ethics through his or her omnipotent knowledge of wholesome ethics.

So far under the model of sophistical education of ethics we have been analyzing the pros and cons of those models which blatantly confuse teaching wholesome ethics with teaching ethical or moral values. If we consider carefully ethics teaching and its models, we shall find that it has been a recent affair starting only in the eighties. We have seen that in India and elsewhere ethics education in the schools and colleges have been encouraged to find out appropriate models to counter what is known as a 'moral degradation'. Apart from this, we have also started taking care of a number of value-laden practical issues in professional life. Another reason being the rise of several ethical questions emanating from technological revolution and environmental concerns. However, sharp disagreements among thinkers could be seen regarding the methodology of education than what were the ethical concerns. The controversy grew sharper when we felt the need of ethical education in schools. We had a glimpse of this problem while we were discussing the validity of indoctrination, pure pedagogy and anagogy in schools. We should be careful about our prospective analysts because not only they have a relatively immature mind they have also an uncorrupt mind which may be incorrigible when it is corrupted beyond control. In secular democracies like India we will also realize that it is altogether a difficult proposition to live a morally charged social life when diversity is manifested so prominently that it endangers the basic unity of the society. It is also difficult to keep a moral balance when population has exploded to an unmanageable proportion giving rise to a number of social, political and economic crises.

In this climate of strife and strain, the urge for ethical education saw emergence of a sophistical model in such education. As we go on explaining it now, our earlier general discussion shall enable us to know why such and such models are either sophistical pedagogy or sophistical anagogy, and why such and such models are not the proper ones to be encouraged in ethics education in schools and colleges. A good account of these models is provided by Lismon C. David in his essay "Ethics Educator in School" One such sophistical model is what we call 'character education'. The role of the ethics teacher is to inculcate virtues in the students because that enables them in making a character such that when they enter a professional life and public life of continuous value oriented decision-making they are expected to make ethical decisions rather than the unethical ones. For all this, the teacher or the expert in ethics education is to make it clear about what was right and what was wrong in a given situation while a teacher is engaged in such things, he or she may take the help of anecdotes, stories and enable pupils to understand what these dilemma-situations are and what decisions should be taken or what is morally desirable. This model of ethics education was thought to have an edge over the model of parental indoctrination, leaving absolutely no room for teachers and an edge over the model of value-neutrality of teachers as advocated in the model known as 'value clarification'. But the model of teaching ethics raises a number of questions. First and foremost is, whether or not it is at all sensible to imagine of character building of a person through another kind of indoctrination (by teachers in this case). We raise this question because what it is to build a person's character from school level is not well-defined. Is it that a kid coming to school is a characterless person and should be trained for building a character, or is that one has a better character when taught by a teacher? Is it not true that after being taught values to a class of 30 odd pupils, a lot of them act immorally quite often and those acting morally often act immorally? Now let us assume that after a dose of èthics, we have a moral character. What is the standard of such morality? When do we call a character moral? At what point of a man's life is he having a moral character? How do we judge as teachers that such and such boy or girl has build high moral character? Is conduct the measure of character? The model speaks of decision-making in the face of moral dilemmas as well. Do we think that in an imaginary situation in classrooms the story-telling and responding method is satisfactory to judge that a student is a good or morally good decision-maker in the face of such and such value-laden situation? Does an intelligent or even a common sense reply to a decision-making situation in a classroom guarantee the growth of a moral character? Further the teacher's role is peculiar as well. The teacher is not value-neutral rather interferes in deciding values or imposing values to a decision-maker. The teacher is not merely a story-teller and a game-maker, he or she is an indoctrinator by virtue of the most appropriate omnipotent ethical knowledge possessed by him or her. What is the guarantee of such appropriateness and omnipotence of ethical knowledge? Moreover, even if the teacher accepts limitations, why should we think that through his or her moral intervention he or she has been able to develop moral character and not an immoral character? By using case or a story and explaining what was right and good in one situation, is a teacher successful in building moral character? Or are they able to make a perfect moral decision-maker? No perhaps, because the 'game-situation' will often not fit into a real life situation, and even if it fits, a number of circumstantial factors may be found to be entirely new and quite decisive in case of a decision-making. So pure pedagogy in this game-style is not satisfactory in ethics teaching. Finally was it really ethics teaching in schools and colleges or was it a course in ethical virtues and virtuous decision-making? Is it not true to find out the theoretical reasons for favouring one decision rather than other? Was it not proper to go for a lesson in theories as well? Let us assume that it was proper to do so but what about the justification of real life application of common ethical knowledge and analysis of the theoretical aspects involved in a resolution? One may wonder asking, "do you expect such cumbersome things from our students at schools and colleges?" Impossible and impractical these things are, so why not do something at least to start with in the name of ethics teaching? My answer is, what will be the harm if we stop such sophistical indoctrination in the name of teaching ethics and character building? Well, if we retreat to give it another name, 'virtue education' or 'education of ethical values' we may accept such interesting indoctrination but why call it a model of teaching ethics? It is in no sense a model of teaching ethics. It may be nevertheless a sophistical model of teaching ethical values. So we have two options to choose, either 'character education' is not a model of indoctrinating ethical values or it is a sophistical model of teaching ethics. In any case, it is teaching wrongly so called, and there ends the matter.

Another model has been put forward by Lawrence Kohlberg, known as the *cognitive model* of moral education. Kohlberg proceeds with a methodical and scientific explanation of the stages of moral development in individuals. If we do not take care of such stages of development, we may be completely at loss to apply appropriate methods in morally educating a child. A child for instance has a relatively immature form of moral reasoning and decision-making capabilities, and needs some kind of intervention or indoctrination from a moral authority or authorities. But this has to be stopped (we have seen why should we do so while discussing indoctrination). Indoctrination has to be replaced by a game model but with a difference that we do not nearly create an imaginary or artificial game situation of moral dilemma in classroom teaching, we initiate those pupils having better moral cognition to participate in the resolution of such dilemmas by calling into service the universalistic ethical theories like deontology, teleology and so on.

Here we have not only scope for the better cognition of why such and such theories in resolving such and such dilemmas are better suited over other theories in revolving such and such moral dilemma. So we have a decision-making within decision making because we have a rational choice of theories through critical acumen emanating from moral cognition and an application of the theories in a game situation. And all this done for our gradual growth of moral cognition and moral character. It may well be that when we pass out in flying colours in test like these our minds are so morally trained that it becomes a state of mind to call into service the right moral theory in right dilemmatic situations in real life as well. We gradually become ethics experts, ethics teachers and ethics authorities. Careful readers must be noticing what Kohlberg's model has to say finally. It is a model of ethical engineering, which is clearly sophistical. It allows great deal of pedagogy with a difference nevertheless. The model is however more straightforward in not confusing ethical and moral value teachings with a wholesome ethics teaching because Kohlberg is feeling a need for knowledge of ethical theories, their justification, their nuances, their relative advantages and disadvantages and finally, their application by virtue of a rational choice at right moment to resolve moral impasse. When a teacher teaches all these things, his task of sophistical pedagogy is complete. He believes that he has build up few noble souls. One also wonders about Kohlberg's *a priori historicism* about individuals' moral development. Does he have enough concrete evidences in favour of such findings regarding moral development? Moreover, does he not feel the importance of taking the students right at the heat of the matter, that is, in a more concrete real life situation of moral dilemmas and debates to resolve them? Is it not important to find out for our students how moral views conflict and converge rather than doing some moral engineering in an artificial manner? Is it not important to analyze the logics of the different moral opinions rather than being co-opted with theories and applying them unilaterally and unopposed? Really speaking, we have not taught wholesome ethics to our students without teaching practical ethics, and all this needs a level of cognition. I do not have any sound proof of the development of such knowledge in individuals at a particular age. But what I may say safely is that in so far as we have not started applying ethics in real life and are involved in post-application theoretical analysis, we do not have a moral cognition so importantly needed. So it would dawn on you when you start at an age of maturity not conclusively well defined. I hope it will be a little overdoing at a tender age or even at the high school level. Yet, educators should take a risk and have a go at it at high schools. Any way we should be careful about Kohlberg's attempt at sophistry.

The breakdown of sophistry either in the form of pedagogy or in the form of anagogy, particularly at a tender age or immature level raises more serious problems when we consider ethics teaching for older children. Although to think that wholesome ethics may be bravely taken up at high school level, may not be universally accepted. I think we need not jump into such hasty decision any way. We have to be very careful and involve in a lot of trials before any national policy or even a local policy of ethics education has been shaped properly. We will have liberal people favouring more and more individualism to stress upon an early course in ethics teaching mostly in a game-condition. Or else we may have more careful people trying to do a lot of trial and error with growing children before deciding a course in wholesome ethics. But my concern is different. At any level and following any model, what is crucial is to keep in mind why do we feel the need of such education. If all models keep in mind but one thing, namely, building a great moral character, I think we are trying to achieve an illusory goal because there will not be a point of time in history when a complete social agreement will be lasting about a noble moral character and how it has to be achieved. It will be really cumbersome to draw a list of character making points to check out whether all has been put in a noble character. There will be perhaps not a single moment in history when all will agree that here we have the paradigmatic ethics teaching and then check for all elements while imparting such teaching. If the models aim at something different, that is, enabling people to grow up with a knowledge such that ethical decision-making is made possible in real life situation or in professional life, we come to conclude that only then ethics teaching needs a careful attention but not in the sophistical way in our schools and colleges. Lisman is correct in saying that "Although developing the ability to think more clearly and carefully about ethical issues and to make more effective ethical decision does not necessarily mean that we will improve moral character as we become better equipped with the tools of ethical analysis, we can more comfortably and effectively attach the issues of the day—we increase our sense that we can exercise some thoughtful influence on social policy and make more informed personal ethical decisions. Second, many of us who teach ethics have found that providing students with the opportunity to think more clearly about ethical issues in a controlled public form, indirectly tends to remind students of their fundamental moral responsibilities."[12]

Lisman is also emphatic about the value of the traditional ethics teaching, which according to him has been imparted following a *tried and true approach* in the philosophy department in different universities. He also commends the value of ethics courses being taught in schools, nursing colleges and so on but warns us of watered-down courses. He then comes to what he himself and other like Peter Steves have been doing which is well known as *ethics-across-the-curriculum* model of teaching ethics. Let us come to it now to find whether or not these models are well founded or are sophistical in some sense. When we come to courses offered in different universities, we find that there is a serious drawback in thinking that such courses have been advanced for what we call preparing people for ethical decision making and for making responsibility oriented people. Ethics teaching traditionally has been in fact most of the time a hackneyed affair of directionless pedagogy—most of the time unimaginative and unfruitful (if the fruits are those aforementioned). The main reason is that till 1960s we were least bothered about practical ethics within ethics and a lot of ethicists have been critical about it and reluctant to include it within ethics. So the burden of teacher has been to teach grotesque syllabus of normative ethics and metaethics. So we have been mostly interested in hackneyed pedagogy of the old era. This is not pure pedagogy because most of the time in universities we were not interested in indoctrination save the medieval ages or in much older times, maybe in *gurukulas* or academies or churches. But I shall not rule out the fact that we have been teaching ethics in an 'anagogical' fashion in our universities. We do teach Christian ethics and many other religiously soaked ethics like Hindu ethics in our universities. The best excuse is that these ethics are within normative ethics so we cannot leave them. I know this but what I was trying to bring out how unethically such religious ethics have been taught. The teacher is often himself or herself determined to indoctrinate, or at times when it comes to practical ethics they would take an instance like euthanasia and show how Thomism, Christian ethics, *Vedāntic* ethics can resolve it beyond any doubt (and we have to follow the same route). This is sophistry, ethical engineering and directed pedagogy. Moreover, where is the appropriate zeal in teaching applied ethics in our universities? Everytime we have tried to be serious about it, we have fallen in the trap of hackneyed pedagogy. We have been teaching and writing books on applied ethics in which a theory or theories are explained, justified and differentiated. Further, we have tried to show how a theory or theories can be applied by ethicists to resolve moral dilemmas. If we go on like this we shall discover that in philosophy and beyond (business, nursing and so on) indoctrination or engineering or, better-said, sophistry continues. Yes, students of medicine, engineering and management are almost sure to be cynical about such sophistry in the long run. If we are serious about ethical application and ethics teaching, pure pedagogy, anagogy and practical ethics without a practical venture has to be carefully avoided. We must remember that a full course of normative ethics and metaethics when imparted to our students will not do if we are really striving for the noble goals we have set for us. Let us remember that pure theory cooption is hopeless. It is unfit for our practical life because professional decision-making demands rules framed through "intersubjective corroboration." Hence, when we speak of models of ethics teaching, we particularly speak of teaching ethics in colleges, in pre-professional course and to our professionals in many cases. Then we have to choose the path of a traditional pedagogy aimed at mere theoretical expertise or we have to choose the path of a new pedagogy which involves intersubjective corroboration. We shall come to this model at a proper place. Let us now have a quick look at teaching 'across-the-curriculum' model.

The best way is to follow what Lisman says, "as educators we have a fundamental social responsibility to help our students understand the social and ethical relevance of their discipline. An effective way this can be done is through presenting discipline appropriate case studies embodying ethical dilemmas containing conflicts between values that we accept independently or case studies that challenge the student to applying a broadly accepted ethical principle to a specific issue relevant to the course material... students should be encouraged to take a basic ethics course in a philosophy department. Also it is important that the faculty have some exposure to ethics theory and approaches to teaching ethics. They do not need to be expert in the ethical theory, but it is helpful for them as they conduct discipline specific ethics discussion in their courses".[13] Lisman is saying that our students should be aware of the social and ethical relevance of their subject. What is great in thinking that all is good to read but not to follow? But what has to be followed in different subjects? Lisman says the 'ethical principles' has to be followed when it comes to the specific subject relevant value. For instance, a medical student is expected to go through (not so deeply or extensively) the basic of normative ethics (what about metaethics?) and when it comes to the case of euthanasia, their expert teacher would allow to apply Thomism or Kantianism to resolve moral impasse. There is no doubt, therefore, that our expert teacher although non-interfering and not indoctrinating is a liberal neutral mediator and facilitates debates in the game-situation. So students apply ethics in the sense of applying the most appropriately thought out moral issues. Our readers by this time must be aware of the misconception of artificial application of ethics theories. Lisman is careful about anagogy because he prefers a secular approach to this whole affair. But what he points out is ethical engineering by students themselves assuming they are ethical experts and their teachers are more of super experts helping them out in such a misadventure. After learning theoretical ethics, models of ethical application and ethical teaching, if the students are not aware of the fact that practical ethics makes sense within their subjects (medicine for instance) only in so far as the students has to undertake a basic *social-scientific vocation* of ethical discourse with concerned parties, in the case of euthanasia, with people desiring it, their relations, sociologists, psychologists, theologians, atheists, theists and others to know how moral resolution takes place, how ethical theories crystallize in moral opinions, how theories become dynamic and sometimes overhauling other theories and how decision-making rules are filtered through corroboration, I don't think teaching ethics is in any way complete. It is rather misdirected pedagogy. Finally, people quickly forget the post-corroboration analysis of the entire moral discourse, which is in reality the real theoretical task before the student. Lisman hints towards an effective pedagogical tool namely 'service learning' which comes closer to this social scientific vocation but it is more of a social service scheme where students investigates an ethical issue like euthanasia in a hospital and talk to such people. But what is needed is to go for a real life discourse with different parties and not merely doing some sort of a benevolent counselling. Hence, the models of ethics-across-the-curriculum and service-learning does convey important truths but is yet not free from sophistry. A little care will take it to what I propose later on.

With this we close examining the sophistical model of teaching ethics. But, we have for us now the *casuistic model* of teaching ethics. Many people believe that in its modern garb it is, truly speaking, applied ethics. We have to take up this misconception now. Readers will be helped by our last discussion on case-based reasoning in a game-situation or in a social service situation when we explained about Casuistry. The extraordinary genius of Immanuel Kant recognized the importance of what he called practical ethics or 'moral anthropology'. When it comes to the question of teaching ethics which includes teaching practical ethics, he recommends for children the most basic form of ethics education known as "moral catechism". In this case an instructor presents some such value-laden cases to young students which they have to resolve in definite words to "feel the progress of their power of judgement". These value-laden cases may be taken from "ordinary life" or from "biographies of ancient and modern times". We have seen that to call this wholesome ethics teaching is a little too much and to expect that we can teach wholesome ethics, is really absurd when it comes to children. But catechism does enter in school education where the need of *moral guidance* is deemed to be more important. However, much different from the cases presented to younger students in the moral catechism, some casuistic questions may be needed for *adults only*, which are more wider questions. Nevertheless in both cases the aim is to provide some moral teaching and moral guidance to our students which enable them in decision-making. Kant accepts that although there can be no rule to teach art of judging, the art of resolution and the art of decision-making, we can do sensible work as theorists and educators to help sharpen the moral knowledge of the students. He is in fact realizing the difficulty in ethics teaching at higher level to all class of students but he is expecting catechism and casuistry having some limited role in enriching the moral knowledge of the students. The greatest problem for catechism and casuistry is that these cannot become means to the moralization of the masses. In reality, moralization is rather impossible and undesirable either formally or in such game-situations. So Kant is aware of the danger of sophistry and accepts that the transmutation of "civilization to moralization" is really difficult effort in the society in which moral agents are destined to live. Here Kant reminds us of the primacy of having enough moral experiences and moral knowledge in the society which enable us to realize the different ways in which value-laden cases are understood and resolved. The person also comes to realize how formal knowledge of ethics is useless unless one involves in this informal or anthropological venture in ethics. But then Kant declares that since formal principles cannot be applied by itself, it needs practical cases for application and resolution, ethics thus "falls into casuistry".[14] This is a straightforward claim about ethical knowledge being applied in practical cases which amounts to casuistry. When it comes to the 'casuistic model' of teaching ethics, we have an idea now that it is a game-situation or case-based application of one's moral knowledge helped by able instruction to learn what one ought to do. We shall take up Kant's 'casuistic pedagogy' later on. Before that, we have to first explain a little more about casuistry.

Casuistry in applied ethics holds that ethical theories are of secondary importance in directly solving moral problems; what is of primary importance is the value-laden case in consideration, allied circumstances, other important details and most importantly, drawing an acceptable resolution. But how we ought to proceed in such resolution is the most debated matter. Casuistry, which was popular to the medieval church fathers, was revived in the 80s by bioethicists particularly by Albert Jonsen. This later on amounted to resolve value-laden biological and medical problems. The great interest among the biomedical scientists was due to the fact that normative theories were found to be too cumbersome to be directly applied in resolving particular cases because they were such generalization which would not be successfully applied in totality in the practical cases of varying types. Those who are interested in applying ethics in biology and medicine would thus find these theories to be of secondary importance.

Albert Jonsen started establishing casuistry with a basic question in mind, i.e., should we conceive of ethics consultants? First, he replied in the negative by saying that no ethics consultant can even call into service one moral theory that indubitably resolves a practical problem of great concern in field like medicine but further he replies the question in the positive by saying that if and only if an ethicist examines all aspects of ethical application, namely, the value-laden practical problem, its difference with other problems, the situation in which problem arises, the people who are concerned about it, their opinion about what ought or not to be done, only then can he or she assume the role of a consultant by summing *all* important factors, taking decisions and prescribing them to the concerned parties because these decisions are not merely pragmatic but have an ethical face. Jonsen thinks that when an ethicist does all these things, he is a casuist and a casuist can be an ethical consultant. The main reason or the underlying logic of such a possibility is that on analyzing the circumstances of a case or what is stark-fact we have any idea about what ought to be done or what is desirable because facts, when they are value-laden, have the disposition to suggest values. This presupposition is essentially Aristotelian in nature because the value element or the desirable element may be derived out of fact by sheer practical wisdom of concerned parties or what is shared understanding sometimes. But what is interesting is to notice that ultimately the consultancy job is not a shared responsibility because it is taken up by an authority, the consultant. But let us not make a mistake that the consultant is a philosopher and none but philosopher because that may be sophistry in a crude form, which Jonsen and others tried to avoid carefully. The ethicist-consultant may be a non-philosopher as well (as was suggested by Aristotle that a person with practical wisdom was fit for moral resolution) but he has to be identified as the one great moral analyzer, moral decider and prescriber of moral decisions. Does this ultimately refer to an ethical engineer? Does this remind us of ethical chauvinism in another name? It does, and therefore, sophistical even in its new vogue.

However, one is ready to point out that what these neo-Aristotelians have been trying to do is not to apply ethical theories artificially by an ethics expert in the name of applying ethics, then is it not true that rather than ethical engineering, it is something different? In common parlance casuists are believed to be anti-theorists. Yet, the truth is that right from the days of Aristotle to Broady, there has been in reality no aversion towards ethical generalization and their real life application. What these so-called anti-theorists did not like was an automatic mechanical type resolution like, "to resolve this problem, call this theory". But the practical wisdom of a consultant is a construction of specialized ethical knowledge of academic normative theories as well which is in fact called into service after a thorough factual analysis has taken place. Facts by themselves do not suggest a value-oriented decision, an analysis of facts by collective mind does suggest such things. But in this whole affair, a deduction of right, ought, desirable or what we call ethical values regarding an issue and the moral decisions taken thereof is taken up by *not collective mind* but *an ethicist consultant*. The *prescribing authority* is the one who by virtue of his practical wisdom is better placed than other parties, whose practical wisdom being devoid of knowledge of such theories are not fit to enter into such deductive as well as prescriptive act. There is a need of division of labour no doubt, which is quite repugnant. Why on earth should an ethicist consultant be better placed in decision making and prescribing? Why should there be such nagging respect for normative theories and for such ethics? This will not in any way prevent our casuist friend to avoid sophistry. The casuists have also forgot in the mean time that one value of their theoretical training, the academic value (if not applicative value) of analyzing the entire analysis of value-laden facts and their resolution by collective mind amounts to know the dynamics of ethical theories. One thing is for certain, if we avoid this task and if we forget to train up people how to perform this task, teaching wholesome ethics as well as applying ethics loses all meaning. We must also remember that when the collective mind is at work in ethical resolution and decision making ethical theories need not be pressed into service. It would be a great ethical blunder not to look into which theories have been really applied, and for this, not merely do we need the consultant ethicist rather, any interested party or parties coming within the collective may contribute in this theoretical work. So there is no scope for ethical chauvinism here as well.

Many ethicist in contemporary times, particularly taking interest in ethical issues have shown some intolerance towards the casuistry of Jonsen, which has resulted into two major approaches, called the *four principles* and the *communitarian* approaches. But they are hardly any different from the earlier approach. Let us analyze them very briefly. The 'four-principles' approach is a result of the works of Tom Beauchamp and J.F Childress. These thinkers have found after a thorough analysis of the epoch making normative theories like deontology and utilitarian teleology that we may derive at least four 'mid-level-principles' of *respect for autonomy*, *beneficence*, *non-maleficence* and *justice*. These 'mid-level-principles' are thus sufficient basis for resolving value-laden issues and for decision-making when a collective mind applies them at those appropriate situations. This successfully avoids the sophistry of artificial application of normative theories but equally important is to take care of those dilemmas which arise in some value-laden cases when some of us are left to opt for one of these *prima facie* duties and leave others, and others are obliged to choose what conflict with ours. The mark of the collective mind in ethical deliberation is to find a perfect "balance" among principles in such cases. The balance is however possible when our prudence is at its best and we are honouring the conflicting views but caring most for what may be most rationally acceptable. The casuistic element in this approach is clear but it is more of case-based reasoning of what ought to be done through the deductive abilities of consultants. But let us not forget that in the traditional 'from the top model' or what I call 'deductive model' of ethical application, same care was taken. There is really no great difference when we speak of deriving the moral ought in practical cases on the basis of one overreaching theory and what secondary rules or *prima facie* duties that may be deduced from these theories. So the 'four principles approach' suffers from all defects 'from the top model' has which, we have seen, is a clear case of ethical sophistry. One important point before we move on to 'communitarianism'. We wonder why should there be only four mid-level-theories or four *prima facie* duties as mentioned by their thinkers? We must carefully avoid any hasty numerical generalization because we perhaps have no idea about many versions of deontology and teleology or do we imagine we know all of them?

Alisdair MacIntyre and Michel Sandel have helped the progress of another revisionary casuistry in the name of 'communitarianism'. These thinkers are in line of Aristotelian thinking that the act of collective mind or community action and deliberation is what is most important ethical application. It is a kind of reviving the Aristotelian "friendship" in case of ethical application. The individual care for the community and the urge for knowledge is the basis of a good life, which is also the basis of an ethically charged life. McIntyre, Ezekiel, Emmanuel and many others have thus tried to stress that we cannot resolve value-laden issues, for instance, those in biology and medicine until the collective mind in the societies come at a consensus on moral trifles. But the most important element that creeps in this model is unlike Aristotle and most annoying for the casuists is the role of normative theories in such a communitarian affair. The normative theories are believed to be their tools which are used to or are extended at the community situation to achieve the goals of ethical resolution of practical and decision-making mainly by shared agreement. This is not liked by the casuists for its clear advocacy of deduction of moral decision from accepting one overreaching ethical theory. Moreover the individuals within a communitarian effort is a lesser being whose ethical views are not given much honour which is due to it even in a community ethical effort. But we must be clear about in what ways this can be done. In fact if we start honouring each and every ethical theory advocated by individuals in community, we can't possibly reach at a consensus. Then the foremost thing is to first have an agreed consensus on which theory to extend to the practical case. But this is a difficult job to do and may point towards an imaginary deduction of *prima facie* duties on which all agree. This so-called casuistry bears signs of sophistry as far as only some people in the community may be aware of knowledge of ethical theories and not all. But how is the imagined friendship possible? Moreover, one wonders why it becomes so important for us to conceive friendship between only theoretical ethicist and not other persons in a community. The shared moral views of other parties are equally important but that is not necessarily among those having theoretical knowledge of ethics. It is also impractical and not desirable at all.

Much has been said about the casuistic model of ethical application and about its affinity to sophistry. What is clearer is that to call casuistry "applied ethics", is a mistake. Two most important points are, in applied ethics no artificial application of normative theories or mid-level theories are deemed to be necessary and applying ethics does not beg ethics experts or even consultants. Now it is appropriate for us to move to explain what casuistic model of ethics teaching amounts to and why it is sophistical as well. Not much has been advocated by the casuists of the modern times about the way ethics teaching ought to be taken but one may read between the lines to know what it amounts to. But better we should take on concrete example of casuistic way of teaching ethics. We shall take Kant's example for the simple reason that his clear view of pedagogy provides paradigm model of casuistic ethical teaching. Apart from the original works of Kant, I owe much to *Kant's Impure Ethics* by Robert B. Louden. He explains, 'Kant in a set of lectures entitled "On Pedagogy" noticed that within human history or the formation of the human being the three stages to cultivate civilize and moralize and are most important. To enable such formation we need practical educations in three parts corresponding to the three stages mentioned above. These are scholastic mechanical formation with regard to skills formation, pragmatic formation with regard to prudence and moral formation with regard to ethics'. Hence, for moralization within human history, ethics teaching is needed. In fact, three stages are interlinked and so are the three points of education. All parts of education aim at moralization though many individuals are completely unaware of such a higher goal but then we are also sure about Kant's clear commitment that ethics teaching is needed for moral formation in individuals. The goal of ethics teaching is beyond any doubt, and also Kant's inclination towards basic sophistry is clear. But let us not be hasty. Kant in his "Religion within the boundaries of mere reason" further clarifies that "the moral formation of the human being must begin not in the improvement of custom but rather in the transformation of the grounding of a character".[15] Although he makes it clear that this "moral formation" (which is initiated through the transformation of the grounding of a character) should be taken because here we are not speaking about forming something new in the mechanical sense. But he also makes it clear that the 'transformation of the grounding of a character' "must be based on maxims not on discipline. The latter prevents bad habits, the former forms".[16] It seems to us now that "moral formation" is not to be taken as "metaphorical" because Kant's view is very clear. He thinks that through proper education we can penetrate the basic nature of a moral agent, that is, the way in which he thinks and acts. Hence, moral education has an unambiguous aim, the change in the basic way in which one is thinking and acting. However, what ought to be the model or method of such moral education?

Louden mentions that 'Kant is very concerned about establishing such a model of ethics education in his lectures 'On Pedagogy' and in his "Essays regarding the philanthropium". Kant asks every now and then about how should children and adolescents learn about ethics. What methods should parents and teachers employ in trying to teach ethics? What are the proper aims of moral educations?' The best replies have been provided in these matters in the "Methodology" section of the "Critique of Practical Reason".

First of all Kant differentiates between teaching ethics to very young people and to more grown up people because in case of the former, the yet uninformed or the uneducated, a physical manifestation of virtue by means of the "exemplary conduct" of teachers and the "cautionary example of other people" is particularly useful. To be precise, we have seen that "moral catechism" is of great practical value in such cases. But we have also remarked why it amounts to sophistry in ethics teaching. We have also remarked that this is in no way teaching wholesome ethics. In fact, such teaching may be not needed at all. In the long run however as we go along formal education and grow up in this atmosphere of learning skills and developing our practical wisdom, we have to realize that moral education cannot be done only by teacher. Our own reason may be the best teacher in this regard. But no doubt to cultivate such reason we need some education, moral education so to say but how if not in the catechistic way?

In his "Methodology" section Kant enlists two models in this regard the acromatic and the erotematic; "acromatic when I alone teach, or erotematic when I ask questions".[17] Kant is then quick in adding that in moral education erotematic or the question and answer method is clearly preferable because that enables the grown up students to see "that he himself is capable of thinking".[18] This is what Kant calls the "dialogue method" which presupposes more maturity on the part of the students. The teacher often uses this method after the catechistic one. So first we have some sort of indoctrination as well as virtue teaching by teacher and then we move on to Socratic method where more interaction could be allowed. However, even if we are here talking about teaching school children, why are we persistently talking about ethics teaching? We must be sure whether we are aiming at ethics teaching or we are aiming at virtue teaching? If what is ethics teaching in the real sense is too difficult for students then we may allow some indoctrination, sophistry and casuistry but why call it ethics teaching? Let us think coolly. Are we really in a position to teach ethics to school students? What is most encouraging in this regard is to find Kant saying clearly that a purely moral catechism and dialogue needs to be completely untainted by religious teachings. So he whisks off anagogy no doubt even at the immature level. Whereas we in India are particularly worried about doing just this in the name of value oriented education. Thus Kant's "ethical didactics" or ethical teaching through acromatic and erotematic methods is particularly mentioned for school ethics teaching in which we have just seen that ethics teaching ought not be overdoing in ethics rather mostly virtue education, and when we enter the dialogue method, what is needed is a case based dialogue. It is here that casuistry enters.

Towards the end of his moral catechism, Kant holds in the "Methodology" section that "it would be of great value to the pupils' ethical formation to raise some casuistical questions in the analysis of every duty".[19] This is particularly needed when some "tricky" situation trouble our minds. However, Kant thinks that ethics teaching in this method does not really fall under the methodology rather under the *doctrine of elements* because it is not merely indoctrination or virtue teaching or dialogue rather something quite different. Nevertheless, he finally accepts that then ethics teaching may not be so simply stated as educating in didactics because casuistic teaching completes the course. Hence, we find how incomplete a statement it would be to say that catechism and dialogue is what is teaching ethics. In fact the entire contents of ethics may not be so simply taught to our young people in our schools and we need not forget that beyond school teaching pedagogy may enter an entirely new dimension. At a more higher level people are not only concerned about what is good or bad or valuable for himself or for other people, people feel a unique growth of ethical knowledge in them that enables to judge in tricky situations what is generally desirable. This is the basis of person's growing keenness in trifling moral issues in society. But Kant is careful to mention that there can be no particular theory cooption because none is complete to practically judge the desirable, right and good. The main reason being the peculiar and unforeseen circumstances for moral judgment and moral resolution. So he concludes that any art of judgment cannot be taught. This saves Kant from sophistry and ethical engineering but then in his "Anthropology from a pragmatic point of view", he says that "there is nevertheless a great deal that teacher can and should do to sharpen their student's power of judgement". But not so narrowly as to teach what rules ought to be followed rather by taking tricky cases and enticing students' mind what decision ought to be taken. Clearly, Kant has fallen back to the wise teachers to do at least three things. The teacher have to select some such "tricky" situations which becomes most important basis of teaching a part of ethics, namely, practical ethics. Next, the teacher has to arrange a game-situation in which such select issues are discussed at length by giving sufficient liberty to the students' freeplay of moral reasoning. This may create an excellent atmosphere of moral debate and scrutiny of those debates. Finally, the teachers are expected in the important matter of judging the logics of moral debates and filter out those desirable decisions, which come out of the analysis of the shared opinions. Interesting is to notice that peculiar gap between the teacher and the taught remains wide open, the former assuming the role of omnipotent knowledge bearer who is at his or her most important work of sophistry. The teacher has not given liberty to the students to gather 'tricky' issues for themselves. The teacher has not left the moral debates to come to a closure by virtue of moral agreement and the students coming forward to formulate value judgments. Neither has the teacher taught how to analyze the moral debate and what normative theories have been at work. But if you say it is altogether impossible at school level, why call it ethics teaching? Why not drop that term? What great harm will be done if we, the teachers of ethics, are not in the vanity of illusion that we were teaching ethics to transform character of our students and thereby moralize them? The greatest problem is that such casuistic model of teaching is completely unfit at a much higher level, particularly in technical institutions, in case of pre-professional teaching and in case of teaching ethics in philosophy course because a power assuming teacher rather than an able moderator and analyst can never be successful in teaching complete ethics including teaching practical ethics. In fact, for teaching practical ethics we have to go to the practical situations to collect information and even if a moral debate is needed, concerned parties should be brought together to demonstrate to our students what really goes on in a real practical ethical situation. A game-situation consisting of "students and teachers" will not do in such teaching because teaching itself has to transcend the pedagogical boundaries. A *post-pedagogical model* in teaching practical ethics is needed, without which "teaching ethics" is a misnomer. I shall now in the conclusive chapter come to discuss what ethics consist of, what ethics teaching consist of and what model of ethics teaching do I propose. This and much more in the name of the prospect of applied ethics has to be stated clearly, because we have at hand a new pathway to people's ethics.

NOTES

1. Gill, Christopher, "Greek Ethics, Overview", in Ruth Chadwick (ed.) *Encyclopedia of Applied Ethics*, Volume 2, Academic Press, San Diego, 1998, p. 483.
2. Hare, R.M., "Adolescence into Adults", in Hollis, T.H. B. (ed.), "*Aims in Education*", Manchester University Press, 1964, p. 51.
3. Barrow, Robin, *Moral Philosophy for Education*, George Allen and Unwin Ltd., London, 19, p. 202.
4. *Ibid.*, p. 210.
5. *Ibid.*, p. 211.
6. *Ibid.*
7. *Ibid.*, pp. 211-212
8. Joshi, Murli Manohar, "*Philosophy of Value-Oriented Education*", Inaugural Address National Seminar, New Delhi, 2002, p. 7.
9. *Ibid.*, p. 15.
10. *Ibid.*, p. 15.
11. *Ibid.*, p. 19.

12. Lisman, C. David, "Ethics Education in School" in Ruth Chadwick (ed.) *Encyclopedia of Applied Ethics*, Volume 2, Academic Press, San Diego, 1998, p. 183.
13. *Ibid.*, pp. 143-144.
14. Kant, Immanuel, *Metaphysics of Morals*, 6 : 411. I have quoted it from Robert B. Louden's "Kant's Impure Ethics", O.U.P. London, 2000.
15. Kant, Immanuel, *Religion Within the Boundaries of Mere Reason*, in Robert B. Louden's "Kant's Impure Ethics", *Ibid.*, 6: 48.
16. *Ibid.*, 9 : 480.
17. Kant, Immanuel, *Metaphysics of Morals in Robert B. Louden's "Kant's Impure Ethics", op. cit.* 24: 599.
18. *Ibid.*, 6 : 478.
19. *Ibid.*, 6 : 483.

6

A New Pathway to People's Ethics

The most crucial question we now face is whether applied ethics, even if it is understood in terms of "intersubjective corroboration", has a future. The question is a skeptical one as one feels that the prospects of people's participation in ethics as stated in the earlier chapters is really not bright. The main reason is that if applying ethics amounts to the application of our 'common ethical knowledge', it is at best application of our knowledge of social mores, customs, traditional norms, and personal and social virtues and values, which in any way is not applying ethics. It is applying ethics without any established theories and principles of ethics. Better said, 'there is no ethics in applying ethics; there is something else, namely, application of social dogmas'. Moreover, social dogmas are in no sense ethics (which is within philosophy), and therefore, its application does not have a bright future. What we apply in the name of ethics is nothing but our dogma of a 'true morality', which has no future. The future may be rather waiting for its complete rejection as trash. Further to think, that a post-corroboration analysis of ethical dialogue reveals the dynamics of well-known ethical first principles in real life situations is another unfounded belief because nothing but private and public moral sense, moral opinions, moral beliefs, moral dogmas and not ethics has been applied will be clearly revealed.

Is the future of applied ethics I have envisioned so dark? Is there no pathway to people's ethics in which value-laden problems are collectively resolved keeping full faith in theoretical analytic work of discovery of ethical dynamics? Let us first try to resolve the residual skeptical doubts the rest will follow. First, to remind the skeptics, it has been argued at length that in application of ethics, standard ethical first principles like deontology and teleology cannot and need not be applied. Another reminder is that a conception of artificial application of ethical theories presupposes ethical chauvinism and ethical expertise leaving out the option of an involvement of professionals with regard to resolution of moral problems. We have to remind our skeptic friends that a possibility of collective resolution of moral problems in society does not beg moral dogmas and there is a difference between applying common sense morality and applying common ethical knowledge through intersubjective discourse. Our skeptic friends may be nurturing an old dogma in their minds that ethics and morality are just the same. In the common parlance we do not make sharp distinctions between the two because we feel that one may easily replace the other but to do it every time may be a great mistake. We have to understand that as a member of a typically identifiable Indian society some of us might have unique moral opinions tracing back to our social customs, traditions, and opinions regarding virtues and values. We cannot pooh-pooh them for they are constituents of our 'moral being', commonly at work in our wakeful active life. Being a member of a typical middle class Bengali I will hesitate to pull off my trouser and throw my shirt to cool-off in a swimming pool with my wife (equally well-dressed), while our parents watching us may be bemused lot. Our counterpart couples in another part of India or elsewhere while reading this might wonder, 'what is wrong with this?' Therefore, what is wrong, that is, morally wrong to me may not be so for others for I am a 'vector' (or carrier) of a certain 'morality' whereas others are potent carriers of other 'moralities'. However, when the problem boils down to say euthanasia or capital punishment we do not behave merely as 'moral vectors' (and we feel that we should not behave like that). Otherwise, we may be *moral islanders* deciding in favour or disfavour of some such things, which were not ethically permissible. We know that moral islanders may be so cruel as to chop off a women's hand because her fingernails are beautifully painted. Who knows that in a modern society able sons will enjoy the right to inject a lethal drug to their terminally ill father! In fact, cases of euthanasia and capital punishment should not be left to our common sense morality; they need careful "moral dialogue" and not whimsical traditional moral sense to take a rash decision. Let us accept the fact that all moral vectors might transcend rudiments of dogmas to apply their common moral knowledge, which is, the knowledge of desirability, right, ought and dutiful. This brings us to realize that application of our common sense morality does not consider the value of collective discourse leading to ethical decision-making. In cases of ethical decision-making, our moral dogmas give way to interplay of our moral knowledge. In such cases, man as a dogmatic being is transcended by man as an ethical being. In fact in due course of ethical resolution no one is perhaps interested in listening to or following the dictates of our moral sense, which are at best the rudiments of social mores, customs and dogmas and not suggestive to what *ought to be done*. An ethical discourse is to churn our ethical being where we move out of "what is done by us or what people do" and enter into "what ought to be done". This is essentially, "transvectoral" or to be more clear, ethics, unlike morality, when applied, is essentially 'moving beyond dogmas or rudiments of the social norms'. Ethics when applied, unlike morality, is also "transversal" or that ethics essentially cuts the edges of local moralities to become more universal. However, I have said that if we accept the relativists' half-truth, our common ethical knowledge of ought is possible only within a teeming social (or more broadly ecological) interactive life of decision-making. This acceptance does not go against what I now say because our empirical anchor to ethical knowledge is not merely a testimony to either "vectoral" or "islander" morality. In teeming societies, the moral knowledge we gather by virtue of moral experience is not just the same as gathering, "what people do" or "what were done by people". Morality in this sense may be "the present is", whereas ethicality is "the present outlook of a possible ought". If ethicality consists of common ethical knowledge and their application for a resolution of moral trifles, it is also the knowledge of the value of 'transcending' moralities and the value of 'transversality' of knowledge of ought. It is clear that ethical knowledge cannot transcend societies, and what is going on here at the historical, political, economic levels but that does not amount to the same as saying that ethical knowledge is 'what is going on at the social, political and other levels'. In societies, several human and non-human activities are incessant, they influence us, they have a potential to spread their roots in moral and dogmatic being and result into several moral opinions and beliefs. But equally true is that within this empirical milieu we have specific experiences of moral strife and moral disagreement about such established norms or moral opinions; we also have specific experiences of agreement and disagreement about what should be done, a question that transcends 'now' and 'then', and the moralities of 'now' and 'then'. We do have experience of transcending the islander morality to move to transversal ethicality. However, is it not true that ethics cannot be infinitely 'transversal'? Is there any doubt that moral resolution of euthanasia and capital punishment has to consider the typical social settings of a nation? If this were true then we have to fall back on the unique dogmas of societies, and with it, on morality and not ethics. Even in this case, we find that social dogmas and social norms are not applied because within the societies of unique identities the common ethical knowledge, that is, the unique transcending-transversal knowledge of the moral being (the knowledge of the essential ought), is applied. There is a possibility, therefore, that transcending-transversal ethical knowledge assumes a universal character. Nevertheless, that need not be pressed too far because every ecological community has its own identity, its issues bear unique character which should be faced by the moral agents in their own unique settings. Nevertheless, the half-truth of the relativists is realized once again but that does not amount to same as following socio-economic-political dogmas in the name of morality. The conclusion is that ethicality is beyond such dogmas. If this were the case then ethics as a branch of philosophy may be concerned with such transcending-transversal ethicality of people, which is an involvement in practical ethics having pragmatic value. Moreover, such ethics is not bereft of theoretical analytic work or metaethical task as the study of the dynamics of ethical theories, their nuances and logical strength and weakness is important in ethics. Finally, the explanation of standard ethical theories having pragmatic value is a normative venture within ethics, which makes great sense as well. Hence, ethics as we understand it, unlike moral science, is neither study of dogmatic morality of men and societies nor study of divine and metaphysical morality. Ethics as I understand it is a branch of philosophy having the three tasks mentioned above, among which the practical task is the application of common ethical knowledge by the ethical being through intersubjective dialogue. It is here that we realize the value of a people's ethics, which is empirically grounded, and not phoenix but common.

Let us analyze the possibility of people's ethics *vis-à-vis* phoenix ethics—a possibility of empirical ethics *vis-à-vis a priori* ethics. I cannot resist myself quoting Kieffer here. He says, "Clearly, we are in need of an ethic that can clarify moral dilemmas and resolve conflicts... we need to engage in ethical theorizing that is responsive to current needs. Whatever is our role, concerned lay citizen, medical practitioner, scientific researcher, and patient—we need *some principles* to help us resolve the perplexing ethical problems that are thrust upon us in this rapidly advancing technological society. The thesis proposed were is this: Humans develop their ethics by the method of *public discussion* leading to public acceptance of what appears to be right and good and a rejection of that which is judged wrong or bad. Further, our conception of which is ethical, right and good changes in the light of new knowledge and continuing debate."[1] The readers at this point may be reminded of the ethical methodology I was speaking along with the notion of application of ethical knowledge within ethics. Kieffer provides me a useful support but I have to make a cursory remark to what he says. The italicized words in the passage remind us of the fact that Kieffer like moral engineers might be under the influence of an artificial application of standard ethical theories though he says that the application is indubitably discursive. In fact, a number of ethical thinkers are under the engineering influence, which is against the spirit of the basic discursive method. Otherwise, Kieffer went on quite elegantly explaining the virtues of people's ethics or what he calls "public ethics."[2]

Kieffer further brings out an important component of people's ethics (and I agree) that it demands a methodology of ethical application in which evaluation of divergent values in society to come to corroboration regarding values is needed. This is particularly needed for coming to "ought behaviour"[3] or what I call, "transcendental-transversal ethicality". Hence, ethical decision-making, which is the climax of ethical application, consists of logical discourse regarding preferential values and once such preferences are spelt out, one must stick to the consequences of such preferences. It is also needed that ethical decision-making involve choices between divergent outcomes, which is in turn placing divergent values on different outcomes. Ethical application is thus collective enterprise, essentially relative to value-related choice. It is, therefore, that ethical application involves both facts and values. This reminds us of the fact that the ethical, unlike the moral is a way of choosing the ought-value and doing what ought to be done. It is choosing the right and the good and doing to attain the right and the good. Ethics in this sense is related to 'ought behaviour'. However, I have some reservations towards accepting Kieffer's opinion regarding relation between the ethical and the moral. To me the relation between the two is not one of dependence as Kieffer think it to be. He thinks that moral rules function as ethical guides, that is, moral rules serve as basis of judging ethical behaviour. To justify this he takes Henry Aiken's analysis of "levels of moral discourse".[4] Aiken conceives of four levels of moral discourse, viz., the expressive, the moral rule, the ethical principles and the post-ethical. The expressive level is the level of moral belief in which some voluntary human decision or intentional choice is judged for its value based on one's belief system. For example, "I don't believe in euthanasia". The level of moral rule is the 'declarative' level in which some intentional choice is stated in terms of a matter-of-fact, which bears an emotive-evaluative import. For example, "Euthanasia is murder". At the level of ethical principles a definite 'ethical reason' is given, the reason stems out of a clear statement of first principle of morality. For instance, "Killing the innocent under any condition is non-permissible". Finally, at the post-ethical level, a statement of universal principle like "The supreme value of life" is taken as a final basis to fortify the erstwhile claim. (All four examples have been stated by Aiken, Kieffer quotes them.) Based on this we come to know that there is a deductive scheme in judgment of moral values and moral decision-making. What is more interesting to me is to analyze what Aiken and Kieffer say about the intimate dependence relation between the moral and the ethical. They believe that the moral belief and emotive-evaluative statements of common people in society are expressive of 'the moral', i.e., they express what are moral and immoral in the context of what people in such and such society think, decide and do. This is further fortified by the notion of 'the ethical', i.e., the conception of what is right, good and desirable.

Hence, the factual and the dogmatic are justified by the moral and the super moral. However, where is the deductive scheme justifying the ethical behaviour by the moral rule (Kieffer calls it reciprocal and even within a coherent system)? In fact, the rudimentary morality of man as a dogmatic being is expressive of our belief system mingled with the emotive-evaluative but when the dogma comes to justification, it begs the ethical and not the other way round. Even if we consider the fact that the dogmatic man is supreme in this context, his dogmas constitute different systems and not a coherent, dependent (reciprocal) system. However, the transcendent-transversal ethical level is essentially different in man. Do we necessarily justify the dogmas of morality in an ethical discourse? Do we really mean to say that if ethics consists of its practical task where common ethical knowledge is applied in a discourse situation, we tend to justify our moral opinions by the ethical? (It will be a little too much to imagine that in such a situation our moral opinions justify the ethical). Really speaking, to justify the moral dogmas is pointless because our common ethical knowledge essentially transcends those dogmas and such knowledge (as I have said) is not known to be the knowledge of ethical principles in any way by common people. Interestingly even if a trained person is aware of some such ethical principles, in real life application of ethics such principles can never be applied deliberately. Even if some tries to be wise enough and apply some such principles, he or she may soon lose ground in a moral discourse. If he or she is very careful at that, is it at all moral to apply ethics in that way? We have answered it in the negative because that is against the ethical liberty of common people who are able to transcend the moral and able to apply transversally moral knowledge, which is knowledge of "ought behaviour". Ethical chauvinism, apart from the unfounded deductivism corrupts Aiken's and Kieffer's thesis if they pressed it too far. It is not difficult to find Kieffer pressing it too hard. We shall come to it now to find out what should not be done in the name of people's ethics.

The steps of people's ethics are: (a) posing ethical issues or recognition of an ethical problem, (b) evaluating ethical positions based on comparison of the consequences of one's own set of values or to ask, could I live with this? There are other ways of evaluation as well, Kieffer imagines the universalisability, consequentialist and deontological theories as helping aids in this regard, and (c) application of ethical theory, which he says, is "moving from the theoretical to the practical".[5] I have nothing much to say about the first part of the project. I have to remind our readers that here we should be careful about peculiar division of labour imagined by our ethics experts, which is, non-philosophers supply value-laden problems and philosophers applying ethics. Much has been said against such an imagination. Let us now move on to the second part, which is the theoretical part and the last part, the practical one suggested by the Kieffer. In a real life discourse situation, we are asked to imagine any one of the four theoretical aids to evaluate ethical positions propounded by the concerned parties in ethical resolution. Kieffer is certainly not referring to the post-corroboration analysis of the contesting opinions here (which I have said should be done by ethicists after dialogue is over and decision has been taken). It may be at best a kind of theoretical evaluation going on in the mind of the ethicist who has arranged a dialogue and is moderating it to reach its climax. May be the ethicist is trying to constantly correct the opinions of others by pointing towards an apparent fallacy in terms of the theories mentioned above. This would be a little difficult nay foolish thing to do even by wise ethicists because in a dialogue situation he or she will discover that he or she has to accept a theoretical dogma to be true or else all views of the concerned parties demand correction. Given a gamut of principles, no one view would appear to be true. This artificial job is, therefore, not pragmatic. Finally, we come to 'the practical', and Kieffer declares, "moving from the theoretical to the practical, at least three major bioethical positions can be described which present *application of the theories discussed above*".[6] Whatever may be these bioethical positions, we have at hand a model of ethical application in which 'application of the theories' is needed by virtue of ethical engineering. This has to be carefully avoided in people's ethics because that is essentially chauvinistic and impractical. What ought to be done instead of that has been discussed at length in the methodology section of this book.

However, at this point I would like to reflect on what I have said concluding the methodology of intersubjective corroboration. I have quoted Bruce Jennings stating that this methodology is essentially "social-scientific" in nature. However, something has to be said about the social-scientific vocation in ethics, otherwise category confusion will prevail in the minds of many thinkers. Let us begin with what Jennings thinks about "intersubjective corroboration" (although he had no idea of my thesis because it was written much later). Jennings writes, "By different routes logical position and emotivism had both come to the same conclusion, namely, that ethical claims are not subject to rational discussion or to public intersubjective standards of agreement and evaluation. Telling criticisms of these doctrines, and their eventual overthrow, have provided a good deal of the philosophical warrant for the new work in ethical theory that has blossomed in recent years".[7] Enthusiastic Jennings then finds that "the current renewal of moral philosophy has been stimulated by the rise of applied or practical ethical, where various ethical principles and ideals are brought to bear on practical decision-making and the resolution of moral dilemmas in specific institutional settings".[8] He then goes on to find that "For these reasons, among others, new linkages are being formed between ethics and social science at many different levels... I propose to re-examine the role that social scientific inquiry... can and should play in studies of applied and professional ethics".[9]

I have no doubt about Jennings' first assertion and the third one but his second assertion is difficult to accept because he clearly takes applied ethics as application of ethical principles in decision-making through intersubjective discourses. This is what I have been arguing against at length. Kieffer's example shows us that application of ethics makes a sense in the context of theoretical deductivism and engineering. Now Jennings (even though he sees the truth that ethical application needs a social scientific model), is outspoken about the same theoretical engineering misadventure. One has to clear doubts regarding this fact otherwise to speak of a social-scientific model makes no sense. Interesting is to notice that Jennings is aware of the fact that the 'engineering model' has not been liked by many thinkers. However, he thinks that people have overdone with criticism and overlooked the value of the model particularly from the interdisciplinary angle. He states the merits of this methodology, therefore, to show the sense in which ethics needs a social scientific model. The first merit he mentions is that the philosophical experts like experts of other fields (sciences) have the niche to create a "persona for themselves", that is, a unique expertise (division of labour), and this is welcome. Next, the model has helped to show how moral consensus can emerge among individuals at odds. The applied ethicists like neutral but suggestive insurance agents do not propagate a theory and yet enable us to understand the value of one theory over the other. Finally the model is empirically based and, therefore, acceptable as a scientific one.

Let us take up the so-called "merits" of engineering model of applied ethics. To create a "persona" for the ethicists or to assume a unique expert role like scientists is not at all needed because the task of applying ethics is not bound to the philosophers. By virtue of common as well as specific ethical knowledge, the ways of problem selection, questionnaire preparation, arranging a discourse, moderating it, coming to closure and post-corroboration analysis may be done by non-philosophers as well. In addition, when a philosopher or a non-philosopher takes up the task of applying ethics he is not playing a uniquely identifiable social role. The corroborator is neither a role-player nor a role model. Any professional interested in this task may perform it without thinking much about becoming alien. However, there is no doubt that a wholesome ethics training will be needed for the one who undertakes this task, and this may be unique. Really speaking the training of a corroborator is job-specific like any other scientific training. Nevertheless, to accept the fact that we do need philosopher or non-philosopher corroborators (trained) is not to imagine that such experts know all ethical theories and that they are unfailingly adept at applying the right theory at the right moment. A corroboration dialogue is essentially "moody" because you are always confronting a confrontation situation. It is almost like an entropic situation, which nevertheless tends to crystallize opinions about values and value decisions notwithstanding what an expert or a "persona" tries to do from his ivory tower of ideals. Yes, I agree that intersubjective corroboration helps us to reach a consensus regarding ethical matters but not in a "pied piper" manner. Jennings thinks of a "pied piper persona", but it is not the case because the "moody mass" will not allow this. Then why think of a persona? Why try to boss? The ethicist-corroborator has to moderate the dialogue with all wits and intelligence—he has to correct views, as far as it is illogical, he has to draw parallels; he has to criticize, cancel, overrule, adjust everything. However, if you are really not declassed, you do not know how to do all these things in ethical corroboration. It is like rowing a boat through rough waters and not behaving like an insurance agent. Nevertheless, when you have reached destination, you have a 'cool-task' as well. This is typical to a theoretical ethicist but I have said that if non-philosophers want to take up this task as well, he or she ought to learn wholesome ethics (with a risk that no one can learn all ethical theories). Yes, this model of intersubjective corroboration is empirically based like many social sciences and, therefore, not phoenix. Nevertheless, to say that the engineering model being empirically based is equally useful is unacceptable because in reality the empirical is taken over by the phoenix – the ethical chauvinist and the pied piper. The basic vocation of social science is useful in ethical application as far as philosophers and non-philosophers as participants of a dialogue as corroborators, moderators and analysts has to learn the systematic methods of co-operative application of ethical knowledge. It is now that we can answer the phoenix to show what are the basic features of an ethical method, which is in itself ethical. People's ethics is a possibility if the phoenix is defeated—it demands thousand flowers to blossom through a social scientific method grounded strongly on empirical ethics. A new pathway to people's ethics is thus an empirical ethics aided by a social scientific methodology demanding participation of people as debaters and corroborators.

A practical ethics is people's ethics as far as it is helping the society to clarify concrete problems of ethical urgency. It aims at the "well-being" of people. A practical ethics does not assume purely theoretical and speculative contexts in which people live. The real contexts in which we live are agglomeration of a number of concrete aspects posing specific problems to us. In practical ethics, serious ethicist is concerned with the resolution of these problems so that well-being of the masses is made possible. A practical ethics is thus goal-directed; it is directed towards the well-being of people. However, practical ethics understands the limits of people as far as they are not able to fully understand and resolve all the concrete problems in a society. A practical philosopher thus does not shun its responsibility of contributing to the well-being of people but he or she is always careful about considering not all but some specific moral problems needing urgent resolution. In order to act responsibly, a practical philosopher is always at pains to judge which values are to be honoured. In doing so, he or she may be often mistaken but he or she is almost sure to judge that some ways of choosing, deciding and acting are right and good than others. The right and good he comes to realize is not beyond the well-being of the people. Hence, practical ethics always takes a social and empirical footing. It regards the practical investigation of the right and the good in terms of human well-being as supreme. Practical ethics is thus people's ethics as far as it is an empirical investigation into what is right and what is good for the masses or what constitutes to the well-being of people. Coming to understand what is right and good for the masses is possible through an empirical process and through rational reflection.

Applied ethics is thus empirically oriented, if not purely rational, *a priori*, or metaphysical. It is not purely theoretical analytic either. Its empirical orientation enables to realize the ideal. Hence, the ideal is concretely realizable but not at once, not fully but gradually. The gradual understanding or unfolding of the concrete ideal of practical ethics, which is "well-being", is partly due to the inherent relativism in value-judgements in society, partly due to the absolute fixity of rudiments of morality in human psyche and partly due to the extrinsic situations in which we are placed in this vast ecological community. However, the understanding is made possible through application of ethics when we come together to find a way out of dogmatic morality. Hence, applied ethics "transversally" enable us to realize its ideal gradually. It is thus an effort of the people or the collective moral being. It is clear, therefore, that the means to the achievement of the ideal of practical ethics can be an empirical means. It cannot be a phoenix or ideal means. It is due to this that applied ethics needs an empirical method (or means) to achieve the concrete realizable (not realized) ideal of well-being of people. A people's ethics thus needs an empirical method. Naturally, it has to take into account the empirical methods of the sciences, (in this case, the method of social sciences) by selecting value-laden issues, arranging discourse, moderating moral dialogue, coming to a closure and post-corroboration analysis. Practical ethics as people's ethics should, therefore, depend on the method of social science stated clearly in details while we discussed "intersubjective corroboration". To come to the conclusion then practical ethics has to shun the idea of applying a moral principle or some principles by ethicists. The practical ethicists should remember, "a moral principle is a pattern of acting which consists of a set of conditions that constitutes a type of life and in conforming to such a set of conditions, a person tests the capacity of the principle for enriching human life. Although testing a moral principle is an act, or experience, a moral principle itself is not an act or experience".[10] Clearly, coming to understand the concrete (and not phoenix) value of moral principle is gradual and not *a priorily* and intuitively possible at once and absolutely. This unfolding of the practical value of ethical principles is again empirically grounded, i.e., it also depends on the vocation of social scientific methodology, the "intersubjective corroboration". It is perhaps due to this that the post-corroborative analysis of the debates reveals the real dynamics of ethical principles. Ethical principles are not handmaid of pure reason. The whole ethics, as I understand it is not phoenix. A new pathway to people's ethics is thus laid by defeating phoenix ethics.

NOTES

1. Kieffer, G.H., "*Bioethics: A Text of Issues*", Addison Wesley, Massachusetts, 1979, p. 44.
2. *Ibid.*, p. 44.
3. *Ibid.*, p. 45.
4. Aiken, H., "Reason and Conduct" in *New Bearings in Moral Philosophy*, A.A. Knopf, New York, 1962, Chapter 4, Levels of Moral Discourse.
5. Kieffer, G.H., *op. cit.*, p. 55.
6. *Ibid.*, p. 55.
7. Jennings, Bruce, "Applied Ethics and the Vocation of Social Science", in J.P. De Marco & R.M. Fox (eds.) "*New Directions in Ethics – The Challenge of Applied Ethics*", Routledge & Kegan Paul, N.Y., 1965, p. 205.
8. *Ibid.*, p. 206.
9. *Ibid.*, p. 207.
10. Kimpel, Ben, "*Principles of Moral Philosophy*", Philosophical Library, New York, 1974, p. 216.

Bibliography

Aiken, H., "*New Bearings in Moral Philosophy*", A.A. Knopf, New York, 1962.

Ayer, A.J. "*Language Truth and Logic*", O.U.P., N.Y., 1935.

Barrow, Robin, "*Moral Philosophy for Education*", George Allen & Unwin, London, 1972.

Caplan, Arthur L., "Mechanics of Duty; The Limitations of a Technical Definition of Moral Expertise for Work in Applied Ethics", *Canadian Journal of Philosophy*, Supplementary Volume I, 1982.

Chadwick, Ruth, (ed.), *Encyclopedia of Applied Ethics*, Academic Press, San Diego, 1988.

Frankena, W.K., "*Ethics*", Prentice-Hall, New Delhi, 1989.

Gauthier, D., "*Morals by Agreement*", Clarendon, Oxford, 1986.

Gauthier, W.K., "*The Sophists*", Cambridge University Press, Cambridge, 1971.

Hampshire, S., "*Public and Private Morality*", Cambridge University Press, Cambridge, 1976.

Hampshire, S., "*Morality and Conflict*", Basil Blackwell, Oxford, 1983.

Hollis, T.H.B. (ed.), "*Aims in Education*", Manchester University Press, 1964.

Jackall, R., "*Moral Mazes*", Oxford University Press, Oxford, 1988.

Jonsen, A. and Toulmin, S., "*The Abuse of Casuistry*", University of California Press, Berkeley, 1988.

Kainz, H.P., "*Ethica Dialectica*", Martinus Nijhoff, The Hague, 1979.

Kainz, H.P., "*Ethics in Context*", Macmillan, Basingstoke, 1988.

Ken-ichi-Sasaki and Tanehisha Otabe (eds.), XII International Congress of Aesthetics in Tokyo, Japan, 2001.

Kenny, A., "*Ivory Tower*", Basil Blackwell, Oxford, 1985.

Kieffer, G.H., "*Bioethics: A Text of Issues*", Addison Wesley, Massachusetts, 1979.

Kimpel, Ben, "*Principles of Moral Philosophy*", Philosophical Library, N.Y., 1904.

Kurtz, P., "*Moral Problem in Contemporary Society*", Prentice-Hall, Englewood Cliffs, N.J., 1969.

Leites, E., "*Conscience and Casuistry in Early Modern Europe*", Cambridge University Press, Cambridge, 1988.

Logan, Morish, "*The Problem of Defining a Profession*", The Annals of The American Academy of Political and Social Science", CCXCVII, Jan., 1983.

Louden, R.B., "*Kant's Impure Ethics*", Oxford University Press, Oxford, 2000.

MacIntyre, Alasdair, "Does Moral Philosophy Rest on a Mistake?" *The Monist*, Vol. 67, No. 4, 1984.

Marra, M, "*Modern Japanese Aesthetics*", University of Hawaii Press, Honolulu, 1999.

Morscher, Edgar *et al.* (eds.), "*Applied Ethics in a Troubled World*", Kluwer, Dordrecht, 1988.

Munsterberg, Hugo, "*Zen and Oriental Art*", Charles E. Tuttle, Rutland, 1971.

Nowell-Smith, P.H. "*Ethics*", Penguin Books Ltd., Middlesex, 1959.

Ookerji, S.K., "Rajendra Prasad—Some Comments on Applying Ethics", *J.I.C.P.R.*, Vol. XV, No. 2, 1998.

Pahel, K. and Schiller, M. (eds.), "*Readings in Contemporary Ethical Theory*", Englewood Cliffs, N.J., Prentice-Hall, 1940.

Perry, D., *Professional Philosophy*, D. Reidel, Dordrecht, 1986.

Prasad, Rajendra, "Applied Ethics", *J.I.C.P.R.*, Vol. XIV, No. 2, 1997.

Rhees, Rhus, "Some Developments in Wittgenstein's View of Ethics", *Philosophical Review*, 1965.

Schlick, M., *Problems of Ethics*, (Trans.) D. Rynia, Henry-Holt, N.Y., 1939.

Steele, G. and Kirscher, P., "*The Crises We Face*", McGraw Hill, N.Y., 1960.

Stevenson, C.L., "*Ethics and Language*", Yale University Press, New Haven, 1944.

Thiroux, J.P., "*Ethics: Theory and Practice*", Glencoe Publishing Co., California, 19.

Titus, H.H., "*Ethics for Today*", American Book Co., N.Y., 1957

Trusted, J, "*Moral Problems and Social Values*", Routledge and Kegan Paul, London, 1987.

Werhane, P.H. and R.H. Freeman (eds.), "*The Blackwell Encyclopedic Dictionary of Business*", Vol. XII, Blackwell, 1997.

Wilson, B. and Ikeda, D. (eds.), "*Human Values in Changing World*," Macdonald, London, 1984.

Yuktananda, Swami, "*Values and Ourselves*", Vivekananda Nidhi, Calcutta, 1989.

Index